Charles François Du Périer Dumouriez

An account of Portugal, as it appeared in 1766 to Dumouriez

Charles François Du Périer Dumouriez

An account of Portugal, as it appeared in 1766 to Dumouriez

ISBN/EAN: 9783337156824

Printed in Europe, USA, Canada, Australia, Japan

Cover: Foto ©ninafisch / pixelio.de

More available books at **www.hansebooks.com**

AN

ACCOUNT

OF

PORTUGAL.

AN ACCOUNT OF PORTUGAL,

AS IT APPEARED IN 1766 TO

DUMOURIEZ;

SINCE

A CELEBRATED GENERAL IN THE FRENCH ARMY.

PRINTED AT LAUSANNE IN 1775.

> Army, city, all
> Depends on those who rule; when men grow vile,
> The guilt is theirs, who taught them to be wicked.
> **PHILOCTETES OF SOPHOCLES.**

LONDON:
PRINTED FOR C. LAW, AVE-MARIA LANE;
J. DEBRETT, PICCADILLY;
AND ELPH. BALFOUR, EDINBURGH.

1797.

ADVERTISEMENT.

In the years 1765 and 1766, General Dumouriez, then a captain of infantry, made the tour of Spain and Portugal, by order of the Duke de Choiseul, Minister of foreign affairs in the reign of Louis XV.; and it was to that nobleman he transmitted his observations on the mode of attacking and defending Portugal, whose topography does not appear to have been better known to its neighbours the Spaniards, than to the rest of Europe. The Duke de Choiseul having been exiled in 1770, was succeeded by the Duke d'Aiguillon. After the dismission of the Duke d'Aiguillon in 1774 (who was the personal enemy of our Author, as well as that of every one who had obtained the confidence of the Duke de Choiseul) Dumouriez then added to his military observations, the various remarks he had made on the government, politics, finance, commerce, manners, colonies, &c. of Portugal, and the whole was printed at Lausanne in 1775, under the title of *The State of Portugal in* 1776. It is a Translation of that work which is now offered to the public. However, it may be proper to observe, that several articles have been omitted; some of which contained nothing but invectives, and others related either to subjects of little interest, or whose personality must have rendered them offensive to a nation, which, whatever Dumouriez may say to the contrary, is the friend of Portugal. Almost all the distances of places, as stated by the Author, have been rectified; and the greater part of the proper names which he had written in the Spanish, instead of the Portuguese language, have been corrected; many occasional notes have likewise been added: those which contain geographical illustrations will be found of great utility, and it is presumed that the others will prove equally deserving notice.

When this work first appeared, it was read with great avidity, and received from every impartial reader an unsuspected praise, its Author being then unknown; but it displeased alike the Portuguese and the Spaniards. Dumouriez has told them both the truth, without any reserve; his frankness, which too often bears the appearance of rudeness, may sometimes be thought insulting; and the manner in which he introduces his correcting admonitions, is still more revolting than his censure. Both nations, therefore, condemned the work, which certainly is far less difficult than to refute it.

His military observations are acknowledged to have been made with uncommon sagacity, and the Portuguese may derive much useful instruction from them; he has pointed out all the resources with which a fortunate situation has furnished them: the territory which they must defend, he examined with the eye of an able officer; with the same eye that could discover, twenty-five years after, the Thermopyles of St. Ménéhoud (to use his own expression) where, at the head of an inferior and inexperienced body of troops, he stopped the progress of a Prussian army, commanded by one of the first generals of the age.

This work of Monsieur Dumouriez is but little known in this country, whose interests it attacks with great virulence on every occasion; but considering it always as our duty to defend them, it therefore becomes an object of no small importance to be apprized in what manner those interests are attacked. Impressed with this idea, together with the very imperfect accounts of the interior of Portugal, hitherto published, occasioned this Translation; conceiving that it contains much information upon these subjects, which, under the present threatened circumstances of that country, may prove highly acceptable.

General Dumouriez in his Preface, having particularly recommended a Map of Portugal, in six sheets, published by the late T. Jefferys, it should be mentioned that this Map has since been greatly improved; the northern districts of Estremadura, together with the eastern portion of Alemtejo, have not only been corrected, but traced anew from manuscript surveys, made by a distinguished officer in the English army, during the last war in Portugal. All the frontiers, particularly those of the north, have also been rectified, from the provincial maps lately published at Madrid, by T. Lopez.

March 1st, 1797.   THE EDITOR.

CONTENTS.

BOOK I.

GEOGRAPHICAL DESCRIPTION OF PORTUGAL.

CHAP. I.
Division - - 7

CHAP. II.
Entre Douro e Minho - - 9

CHAP. III.
Traz os Montes (or Tralos Montes.) 16

CHAP. IV.
Beira - - - 21

CHAP. V.
Estremadura - - 31

CHAP. VI.
Alemtejo - - - 41

CHAP. VII.
Algarve - - - 48

CHAP. VIII.
Conclusion - - - 53

BOOK II.

THE PORTUGUESE COLONIES.

CHAP. I.
Division - - - Page 57

CHAP. II.
Asia - - - 59

CHAP. III.
Africa - - - 64

CHAP. IV.
America - - - 67

CHAP. V.
Islands belonging to Portugal - 88

CHAP. V.
Conclusion - - - - 97

BOOK III.

THE ARMY.

CHAP. I.
Defects of the Portuguese Army - 103

CHAP. II.
State of the Army. — Infantry, Cavalry, Light Troops, Artillery, and Fortifications 109

CHAP. III.

Generals, the Staff, Officers, &c. Subsistence; the Minister of War - 116

CHAP. IV.

Topography, Rivers, Mountains, Fortified Places - - - 123

CHAP. V.

Historical Reflections on the War of Portugal - - - 134

BOOK IV.

NATIONAL CHARACTER AND GOVERNMENT.

CHAP. I.

Manners of the Portuguese; the Fidalgos; Women; Public Amusements, Dances, Bull-feasts, &c. - - 154

CHAP. II.

Dress, Buildings, Police, Climate, Earthquakes, Country Houses, &c. - 162

CHAP. III.

Justice, Prisons, Tribunals, Councils, Cities, Orders, Archbishoprics, Bishoprics, the Patriarch, Religion, the Inquisition, the Expulsion of the Jesuits, Schism of Portugal - - 166

CHAP. IV.

University of Coimbra, College of Nobles; Literature, Authors, Historians, Poets, Arts - - - 191

CHAP. V.

The Government, the Marine, Commerce, Agriculture, and Finance - 197

CHAP. VI.

The Court - - - 208

CHAP. VII.

A Summary of the History of Portugal . 213

CHAP. VIII.

Anecdotes——John V., Joseph I.; the Earthquake; the Conspiracy; the War of 1762; the loss of the Customhouse by Fire; the Death of Graveron; the Revolt of Brasil - - - 223

CHAP. IX.

Political State of Portugal - 260

CHAP. X.

Count d'Oeyras - - 265

THE AUTHOR'S PREFACE.

The Title of this Book proves with what ease it is composed—a Work of this kind exacts from its Author neither strict adherence to chronology, method, comment, analysis, eloquence, nor imagination: to speak the truth is all that is required of him: the severest censor has no right to demand more. My Work is a picture, which I colour to any height that suits my idea; if the colour be but true to nature, the strength or weakness of the tint make no difference in its merit; my title is then exact.

From the circumstantial histories of Portugal I have selected some traits,* to throw light upon the national character, and to elucidate my observations upon the present state of the monarchy. A minute detail of facts does not come within my plan.

* History of Portugal, in French, by La Clede, in 2 volumes.

I wish to paint Portugal as it was in 1766: and to my surprise and satisfaction, I find it so little known, that my book will possess completely the merit of novelty.

The intimate connections of Portugal with England, its riches, situation as a maritime power, the horrible convulsions of nature that have in this age shaken its very foundation, the wars it has been forced into, and above all, the transcendent genius of its Prime Minister,[*] ought to call forth the curiosity of all travellers, and excite those that visit its shores to acquire and communicate information on so interesting, and, I venture to say, so unknown a country.

The English travellers, those diligent observers of men and things, seem to have neglected Portugal, or to have despaired of finding in it any object that could repay their trouble, or satisfy their spirit of philosophic research. None visit Portugal but mercantile men, and those absorbed in commerce, confined

---

[*] Marquis of Pombal.

to their desk or exchange, see no place but Lisbon and Oporto, and live entirely among themselves; they, therefore, can obtain but a scanty knowledge of the country.

The Spaniards, though they have a thousand motions of policy, rivalship, and hatred, to urge them to a scrupulous examination of the neighbouring kingdom, are yet more indifferent than the English. They have no map of it, no plan of its fortresses, no account of its armed force, its resources, or of the character and temper of its inhabitants: if such exist, it can only be within the impenetrable scrutoires of ministers, out of which not even the exigencies of war can draw them. It must be fresh in the recollection of many officers how, in the campaign of 1762, while the army was encamped at Zamora, with the intention of penetrating into Portugal, the General, Marquis of Sarria, stood in his hall surrounded by his staff-officers, like the figure of perplexity and diffidence, craving information concerning the roads of Portugal, from persons as ignorant as himself;

how one man had heard from a pedlar, that between such towns the highways were rugged; another had been told, by a lady in Valladolid, that other roads were passable or impassable; all was guess and hearsay; no plan of a campaign was formed, because there was no topographical knowledge; and yet, at that very time lay, buried in dust and oblivion in the public offices, the Memoirs of the great Duke of Alba, the Duke of Ossuna, Don John of Austria, and the Marquis of Bey; the maps and surveys made by their orders; and the plans of Nicholas de Langres, a French engineer, drawn in 1640. The war of 1762 has not produced even a tolerable map; and Portugal is as little known to the Spaniards, in a military view, as the deserts of Arabia.

Thomas Jefferys published an excellent map of Portugal *.

The French, so remarkable for their curiosity, vivacity, boldness, and acuteness of remark; who make reflections and write upon

* An improved edition was printed in 1790.

all subjects, have nevertheless left Portugal untried; content, like other travellers, with a sight of Lisbon and Oporto, they have given us some speculative pamphlets on the commerce of those cities, but have not extended their view into the heart of the kingdom. The French officers, who served as auxiliaries in the Spanish army, saw too little of the country to attempt a description of it; and were besides so disgusted with the ridiculous conduct of the military measures, that their reflections may be more justly considered as bitter satires upon their friends, than criticisms on the operations of the enemy.

One great cause has powerfully operated towards the neglect with which Portugal has been treated by writers and travellers, and that is, the extreme sloth and apathy of its inhabitants; they neither travel, write, nor communicate with foreign nations. The wretched accommodations and bad roads of their own country, and of Spain, may be admitted as their excuse; but why not visit England, their ally?

why not profit of their easy communication by sea with all the world, to know what is passing in some parts of it, and to draw its attention once more to a nation which a few centuries ago astonished mankind by the most valuable discoveries, and brilliant conquests?

Strange to say, its government forbids the exertion; while Denmark, wisely steering clear of the contest, sent its young officers to learn their hazardous trade under great generals, Portugal recalled those subjects whom zeal for glory and instruction had enticed from their homes.

This cloud of oblivion which covers Portugal, this national stupor, stamps a value on my Work; which I shall endeavour to enhance by impartiality, and a steady adherence to truth.

ACCOUNT, &c.

BOOK I.

GEOGRAPHICAL DESCRIPTION OF PORTUGAL.

CHAPTER I.

DIVISION.

THOSE persons who take up a book with a wish to be instructed, will peruse with eager attention the geographical details which are necessary for understanding it, while the same dry statements frighten him who reads only for amusement. I have endeavoured to please both kinds of readers; the former, by my scrupulous exactitude, the latter, by an assemblage of anecdotes and remarks, which will enliven the page, and dispel the gloom. I have given a state of the population of Portugal, not to be met with in other books. Without having verified the account, and seen the vouchers, it is scarce possible to believe that its six provinces can bring forward so many inhabitants, yet the statement is indisputable; and there is room for double the number, without being distrest for sustenance: in the time of the Romans, they nourished more than five millions of inhabitants, and the glorious age of Don Emmanuel reckoned up at least four millions.

The whole extent of Portugal is about three hundred and forty British miles in length, and from one hundred and thirty to one hundred and forty in breadth; it is therefore five times less than Spain. But the advantages of its situation, the assistance of England, the weakness of its enemy, the impervious nature of its approaches, and the number of its strong holds, will always preserve it from the ambition of Spain, were all the rest of Europe to remain an indifferent spectator of the conflict. With these weapons, it will always baffle the efforts of the Spaniards.

Portugal is divided by geographers into six provinces, three of which form the department of the north, viz. Entre Douro e Minho, (between Douro and Minho) Traz os Montes, (behind the mountains) and Beira; the remaining three compose the southern department; viz. Estremadura, Alemtejo, (beyond Tagus) and the kingdom of Algarve.

CHAPTER II.

ENTRE DOURO E MINHO.

The province of Entre Douro e Minho is bounded on the north by Galicia in Spain and the river Minho; on the east by Traz os Montes, from which it is separated by the mountains of Santa Caterina and Geres; on the south by Beira, from which it is divided by the river Douro; on the west by the ocean. Its length is above sixty miles from north to south, its width about forty, from east to west. In proportion to its extent, it exceeds every other province in the number of inhabitants.

In it are two cities, Braga, the capital, and o Porto; twenty-six towns, or walled burghs; the principal of which are Viana, Guimaraens, Ponte de Lima, Villa de Conde, Caminha, Monçao, Barcelos, Valença; it reckons two cathedral, five collegiate, and more than five hundred parish churches; it is watered by many rivers, which distribute fertility, and are crossed by more than two hundred stone bridges.

The chief productions are corn, wine, oil,

wool, and flax; living is cheap; game and fish abound.

It is divided into six jurisdictions; viz. three royal, called Corregedorias,* and three feudal, called Ouvidorias.

Guimaraens is the first corregedoria, extending over four towns; its district is large and populous, containing 124,000 souls. The chief town stands between the rivers Dave and Visela, three leagues from Braga; it was the residence of the early kings of Portugal, the birth-place of Alphonsus Henry, who first assumed the regal title. Here is a collegiate church; the canons possess great riches, and belong to the higher class of nobility. In the fish-market is a ruined church, dedicated to St. James, which was in Pagan days the temple of Ceres; the town contains 5000 inhabitants, and is defended by an ancient castle, built on an eminence.

The second corregedoria, Viana, consists of nine towns; the most considerable Monçao and Ponte de Lima. It numbers 98,000 souls.

* *Corregedor* is the name given to the chief civil magistrate appointed by the king; and *Ouvidor* the name of the subordinate magistrate appointed by the lords of the respective towns or districts. T.

Viana is situated at the mouth of the Lima, with a harbour once very practicable, but of late years the sand banks have accumulated, and no vessel of burden can get in; it is well built, in an agreeable country, with about 7000 inhabitants; Alphonsus III. was the founder in 1253. The castle of St. James, raised on a neck of land, with bastions cut in the rock, defends the entrance of the port.

Ponte de Lima boasts of great antiquity, attributing its foundation to the Greeks; it stands on the Lima, ten miles above Viana, and is a neat little town, of about 2000 souls. Monçao was built by Alphonsus III. about nine miles from Valença, on the Minho; contains only 700 persons; the fortifications might be made very respectable with moderate repairs.

The third corregedoria is o Porto, ("the Port,") or Oporto, or Porto, in which are one city, three towns, and 100,000 inhabitants; next to Lisbon Oporto claims pre-eminence, in point of value, over all Portugal; its port, at the mouth of the Douro, is famous for its traffic, which has drawn to it a great concourse of people, especially within the last thirty years; the effects of the tremendous earthquake of 1755 were but little felt here;

foreigners swarm at Oporto, and carry on its trade; the English are the most numerous. In 1732 this place contained only 24,000 inhabitants, the number is now nearly double*: it is open and unfortified, except towards the sea, where two forts have been built. Living is cheaper than at Lisbon, society more agreeable. After the earthquake, the court had thoughts of removing hither. The inundations of the Douro frequently cover the quays and low quarters of the city.

The first ouvidoria is Barcelos, containing seven towns, and 50,000 souls. The town of Barcelos gives title of count to the house of Bragança; it stands nine miles from Braga, and has a collegiate church, but only 1500 inhabitants.

The ouvidoria of Valença embraces three towns, of which the principal one, Valença, was founded on the Minho by the veteran soldiers of Viriatus; it was once regularly fortified, but the works have long been in a state of ruin; the present minister has directed them to be restored; Tuy, the frontier town of Galicia, is not out of cannon shot from Valença,

---

* In 1705, it contained only four thousand. T.

which gives title of marquis to the house of Vimioso. The population of the district does not exceed 26,000, that of the town amounts only to 900 souls.

The ouvidoria of Braga includes that city only, and 34,000 inhabitants, of whom 12,400 reside at Braga, which is said to have been founded by some Greeks returning from the siege of Troy; it stands in a pleasant plain, distant seventeen miles from the sea, watered by two rivers; the Cavado on the north, and the Deste on the south side. This city was an important station in the days of ancient Rome, and still shows, as proofs of its former grandeur, an aqueduct and a ruined amphitheatre; it is well built; the see of an archbishop, to whom its lordship belongs, who assumes the title of Primate of Spain, as filling the most ancient episcopal chair in the peninsula. Five councils have been holden here, and 114 prelates have worn its mitre, some of which are held in high repute for sanctity and learning; the famous Bartholomew of the martyrs at their head.

The six jurisdictions of this province contain, according to the last rates, 504,000 inhabitants, who are in easier circumstances in general, as being more industrious and resolute than those of the other provinces. They are of a handsomer breed, robust, and agile, frank and loyal subjects, and esteemed the best foot soldiers in the kingdom.

Entre Douro e Minho is exposed in time of war to nothing more dangerous than slight desultory attacks on the frontiers, which towards Galicia are well covered by the Minho, and cut through with innumerable defiles and impenetrable dells; its people are brave, and animated by a most ardent hatred against the Castilians. There are besides some fortresses, especially along the banks of the Minho, such as Valença, Villanova, Lapela, Monçao, and Melgasso. Many large streams, that run across the frontier from the deep recesses of the mountains, contribute greatly to the strength of the country; every river that waters the inner parts of the province (viz. the Lima, Neyva, Cavado, Deste, Dave, and Grisoner) directs its course from east to west, and consequently forms natural points of defence, and posts which, joined to the steep mountains, must render an irruption on this side very difficult and hazardous. Near the source of the Lima towards the north, the entrance is wider, but there also are many excellent posts along the

Vazzeas, viz. Tiar, Paradela, Forte da Estrica, and Portela de Homem. On the east side, the province is separated from Tras os Montes by the chain of Geres, Santa Caterina, and Maram, which is very hard to pass, and very easy to defend, by breaking up the ways, making abattis, throwing up breast-works and redoubts; upon the whole, this province, though tempting from its riches, is in little danger: the Spaniards have never made any great impression upon it; and so well is it calculated to defend itself, that its safety is entrusted to its own militia, except two or three battalions placed in the garrison of Oporto. Such hitherto has been the arrangement, which has sufficed for the preservation of Oporto against hostile attacks. The badness of the roads, the quantity of wood, and the abruptness of the mountains that hang over this city, inspire it with confidence of security, and perhaps ought rather to excite apprehensions, if the Spaniards understood the art of making war with light troops.

CHAPTER III.

TRAZ OS MONTES, (or TRALOS MONTES.)

THE province of Traz os Montes is so denominated from its situation with regard to Entre Douro e Minho, from which it is disjoined by the ridge of Maram and Geres on the west side; to the north is Galicia; to the east the kingdom of Leon, and to the south Beira. Its surface is mountainous and dry, but near the rivers, the narrow slips of plain are populous and fertile. It comprehends two cities, Braga and Miranda, and fifty towns; reaches about eighty-six miles from east to west, and between sixty and seventy from north to south; is divided into two corregedorias and two ouvidorias.

The corregedoria of Torre de Moncorvo contains 26 burghs and 45,000 inhabitants. In 1762, the Spaniards placed a detachment here, which did a great deal of mischief. As they marched to attack it, they took it for granted they were to meet with a fortified town, and it was said that a corps of 8000 Portuguese were to defend it. The astonishment of the

Spaniards equalled their ignorance, when they found Moncorvo was but a sorry village, that, for the last hundred years, had had neither wall nor gate, nor had it seen a soldier stationed there during all that time.

The corregedoria of Miranda contains an episcopal city, 12 burghs, and 24,000 souls. Miranda was fortified, but in the ancient style, when the Spaniards came to invest it in 1762; a powder magazine blew up accidentally, tore the castle to pieces, killed 600 men of the garrison and of the town, and laid the place open to the enemy. The same disaster had befallen it in the wars for the Spanish succession. It is impossible to re-establish this fortress to any good effect, as it is commanded by the heights; yet a post here would be a great barrier against Leon, and be an advantageous outlet for an invasion of Spain with light troops.

The ouvidoria of Bragança comprehends a city, 12 towns, and 75,000 inhabitants. Bragança is the capital of the province, but the bishop's see has been removed to Miranda; it stands in a narrow plain, near the banks of the little river Fervença, only nine miles from Galicia, and Leon. Its founder is said to have been Brigo, the fourth monarch of Spain, in fabulous times;

but it has another full as honourable and more probable. A colony was settled here by Augustus, and, in honour of his great-uncle, called Julio* Briga. It bears the title of dutchy, and belongs to the reigning family. Here are some good manufactories of silk, velvet, and grogram. Its walls are antique, defended by sixteen towers; the castle pretty strong. In point of relative situation to Spain, it resembles Miranda, and contains 2700 inhabitants. In 1762, the Spaniards lost above 4000 soldiers in an hospital they had established here.

Chaves is the most considerable town of the province, and the residence of the commander in chief of the northern department. Vespasian first settled it, and built fine baths here, of which some fragments remain to this day. Over the river Tamega is still to be seen a very remarkable bridge, erected by Trajan. There are fortifications, but all difficult to defend, being, as all the rest in the district are,

---

* This is a mistake; the town of *Juliobriga*, belonging to the *Cantabri*, was situated at the foot of the mountains where the Ebro takes its source. Jefferys's map calls Braga *Brigantium*, which is likewise an error, tho ancient name of that city being *Bracara Augusta*. Betanços in Galicia is the ancient *Brigantium*. T.

commanded by eminences. The royal family possesses the seignory. It was from Chaves that the Spanish general detached, in 1762, a corps of 3000 volunteers, that were to march to Oporto as avantcouriers of the army; Alexander Oreilly*, now a lieutenant-general in the Spanish service, in high esteem, was put at their head, and was to have been supported by other parties. He pushed on as far as Villa Real without meeting with any resistance; but there he learnt that the peasantry was arming, and that the defiles were dangerous, upon which he turned back, and made a very disorderly retreat; at Villa Pouça, and as far as Chaves, the peasants harassed him exceedingly, and had the glory of driving him back with loss and disgrace, though their number did not exceed 600, nor had they a single military man with them. This feat was highly celebrated in Portugal, and the particulars of it repeated with great pride. The failure in this operation occasioned the retreat of the Spanish army to Zamora, the siege of Almeida, and all the confusion and blunders of the cam-

---

* Famous for his ill-fated expedition against Algiers in 1775. He died a captain-general in 1791. T.

paign. Portugal was at that time without troops and planet-struck; had the army advanced rapidly upon Oporto it must have taken it without firing a gun. Great resources would have been found there, both in money, stores, and provisions, and an excellent climate; the Spanish troops would not have perished as they did, with hunger and want of accommodations; the face of affairs would have been totally changed.

This province is not worth an attack in a war between Spain and Portugal; it is even dangerous for the Spaniards to penetrate into it, as they found to their cost in the late war; 40,000 men advanced to Chaves, Bragança, and Miranda, without magazines or provision of any sort, and about a fourth of their number died there of sickness, hunger, and want, without a single point being carried in favour of the general attack upon Portugal.

CHAPTER IV.

BEIRA.

The province of Beira is the largest in the kingdom; it borders to the north on Entre-Douro e Minho and Traz os Montes; to the east on Leon and Spanish Estremadura; to the south on the Portuguese Estremadura and Alentejo; and to the west on the Atlantic. Its length eighty-two miles, its breadth above one hundred; is divided into six corregedorias and two ouvidorias; contains four bishopricks, viz. Coimbra, Viseu, Guarda, and Lamego; four cities, and 234 little towns, with 560,000 inhabitants: in some parts the country is fruitful in wheat and rye, and abounds in game, and sheep, fish, and fruit; in others, an universal sterility reigns. The climate inclines to cold, on account of the quantity of mountains. In some districts near the sea Beira produces excellent wine and oil, as good as that of Andalusia; the English buy most of it, as well as its lemons and oranges. This province is divided into upper and lower by a lofty ridge, called La Serra de Estrella.

The corregedoria of Coimbra contains one city, many burghs, and 150,000 souls. Coimbra (Conimbriga) was built by the Romans, about 300 years before Christ, on a spot distant one league from the present city; but the Alani having destroyed it, Ataris king of the country raised it anew in 415, on the banks of the Mondego. Coimbra is celebrated for its university, founded by king Denis, which has seven professorships for divinity, seven for canon law, ten for civil law, seven for physic, one for mathematics, and one for music. The city has a fine bridge over the Mondego, and musters 10,000 inhabitants, besides 4000 students. The bishop is titular Count of Arganil.

The ouvidoria of Montemoro Velho contains 30,000 inhabitants; the ancients knew it by the name of Medobriga*. This town stands on the banks of the Mondego, thirteen miles from Coimbra, and has 4000 inhabitants. Aveiro, comprized within this district, is a seaport that improves daily, and with a little expence, may

* Another mistake: *Meidobriga*, not *Medobriga*, was situated near mount *Herminius*, about seventy miles to the south-west of Alcantara; its remains are called now Armenha. T.

become excellent: its situation, and the fertility of the environs, have allured to it many strangers, English especially, who carry on a considerable traffic in oil. This is the chief town of the dutchy of Aveiro, and reckons 4400 inhabitants.

The ouvidoria of Feira contains 42,000 souls; its town, with title of county, is supposed to have been founded by the Asturians, in 1000, at the distance of twelve miles from Oporto. It offers nothing worthy of notice.

The corregedoria of Viseu includes an episcopal city, and 22 small towns, with a population of 95,000 souls. Viseu is situate in the centre of the province, between the waters of the Mondego and those of the Vouga; it was founded in the time of Sertorius, by the proconsul D. Brutus, and called Vicontium*. Two towers yet remain, of Roman construction, on which appear the eagle and the names of Flaccus and Frontinius, probably the architects or overseers of the building. But the greatest cu-

* In Jefferys's map it is called *Verrunum:* some Portuguese authors, I don't know upon what ground, pretend that it was founded by the *Turduli,* 500 years before Christ, under the name of *Vacca,* and named afterwards *Vicus Aquarius* by the Romans. T.

riosity is the tomb of the ill-fated Gothic king Rodrigo, who, if we were to credit the groundless legend of the Portuguese, escaped from the battle of Xeres and the destruction of his empire, became a monk at Viseu, and died long after in dolour of sanctity.

The corregedoria of Lamego comprehends an episcopal city, 33 towns, and 60,000 inhabitants. Lamego stands on the Douro, in a plain surrounded by mountains. Its origin is carried back to some fugitives of Laconia, 360 years before our æra; Trajan restored it by the name of Urbs Lamacænorum*. Notwithstanding many disasters, which at various periods have befallen it, the inhabitants, in number 5000, possess considerable wealth. Here is a great annual fair for horned cattle.

In the corregedoria of Pinhel are 55 towns and 70,000 inhabitants. The town is fortified after the old fashion, and contains nothing remarkable. Almeida is the principal place of the district, and the strongest fortification in Portugal. It has six royal bastions of stone and as many ravelins; that fronting the river

* Its more ancient name appears to have been *Lama*, though Ptolemy attributes that town to the *Vettones*, instead of the *Lusitani*. T.

Coa, which runs at the distance of a mile, is of a noble extent, and furnished with a *cavalier*, for the purpose of commanding the circumjacent country: there is a good ditch and covered way. Nearly in the centre of the town, on a lofty mound, stands a castle, famous for its strength, and magazines bomb proof; within its walls are wells, and at a small distance a fine spring of water. The number of souls in the town 2500. The siege and surrender of this place to the Spaniards in 1762, caused the loss of a great deal of precious time, provisions, and treasure, without obtaining any important end; the same thing will always happen when the same plan of a campaign shall be adopted; for the conquest of this fortress is of no importance with regard to the real frontier of Portugal; the conqueror of Almeida is not more certain of penetrating to the heart of the kingdom, than he was before he took it. An absurd inveterate prejudice urges us often to sacrifice men and money before useless ramparts, merely because the ancestors of our enemies have been such systematic fools as to fortify them.

The corregedoria of Guarda contains an episcopal city, 30 burghs, and 7000 souls. The city of Guarda was founded in 1199, by king Sancho I. near the head of the Mondego, and at the foot of the Serra da Estrella; its walls are of stone, and turreted; its castle overlooks the plain. Its population 2700 persons. The prelate resides at Castelbranco. The plain of Guarda is much above the level of the whole province, and commands it completely; it would be an excellent camp for 20,000 men. Lord Galway in his Memoirs decides that it is by far the best post that the Portuguese can take for the defence of Lisbon. It has before it Sabugal, Penamacor, Castelbranco, &c. for advanced stations, commands the defiles that lead from them, and is defended by woods and swamps in front; while the river Zezere covers its right flank: thus it would protect all Beira, and the towns both of the Tagus and the Douro.

The corregedoria of Castelbranco is composed of 22 burghs, and 40,000 inhabitants. The town stands between two streams, the Liria and the Ponçul, fifteen miles distant from the Tagus; it is fortified with a double wall, seven towers, four gates, and an old castle once formidable, and contains 4000 inhabitants. Idanha a Nova (New Idanha) is a burgh, so rich and abounding in provisions, that the Spanish army lived upon what it furnished for a whole month. The knights of the order of Christ have the seignory. Penamacor, erected by Sancho I. is on an eminence thiry-five miles from Almeida, and on the Spanish limits; its castle commands to great advantage the whole range from Castelbranco to the Coa; but its fine position for defence has not been improved by any works: 2500 inhabitants form its population. The conquest of Beira can only be achieved with ease through the Portuguese Estremadura and the plain of Leiria. To an enemy marching from the Tagus towards Coimbra, the province becomes an easy prey, as its natural defence of mountains, ravines, and defiles, which guard the frontier, are by this line of march turned and rendered useless. A passage along the banks of the Tagus is easily forced, for there the walls and fortresses are in a state of neglect and ruin.

The Portuguese, though guided in general by very erroneous principles in their wars with Spain, seem, however, to have blinded their enemies as to the real point of attack; indeed, to all appearance, they themselves are completely ignorant of it, for they are now working, at an enormous expence, and great activity, at the repair of that most useless fortress, Almeida; they are also lavishing great sums upon the fortifications of Elvas, in order to deceive the Spaniards, and induce them still to look upon those as the keys of Portugal; but they do not endeavour to find out what other openings the enemy might push through; a line of posts might, with ease and with little expence, be formed along the mountains and the course of the rivers, which, by a very simple method of fortification and defence, would cover Lisbon and Oporto from insult. But to state the matter fairly, the Portuguese government is not so much to blame, as it knows the character of the Spaniards, and has reason to think they will always esteem Almeida a place of infinite consequence, and its reduction a sufficient reward for a whole campaign; that they will always commence their operations by the invasion of Beira, and by that prejudice keep the war at a distance from both Lisbon and Oporto, the loss of which would endanger the whole kingdom.

The reduction of a few places, which at the peace must be restored, whatever men and money they may have cost you to take and preserve, are nothing to throw into the balance of a negotiation; this truth the French have found out after every German war. In the present state of things, Portugal depends upon Spain's adopting a false, expensive, undecisive system of warfare—woe to Portugal if Spain should discover its error, and take advantage of Portuguese ignorance and negligence.

To return to the siege of Almeida. If the Spaniards undertake it, this project detains them far from Lisbon, gives time for decision in the Portuguese cabinet, and for the arrival of English succours. The fortress, if well defended, may waste a whole campaign, and when taken will be of little use, by reason of its distance from the centre of operations; meanwhile the enemy may take post in the gorges and defiles of Beira, entrench themselves in the fine camp of Guarda, and so ward off from Lisbon the blows of war, against which, in fact, they ought principally to be directed. I even affirm that were all the provinces of Portugal to fall into the hands of an invader, if Lisbon and Oporto be not reduced, the aspect of the war would not be more changed, as far as regards a negotiation for peace, than if nothing had been done; I therefore am confident that the surrender of Almeida, instead of promoting, really retarded the progress of the war. After taking that fortress, the remainder of the campaign was spent in uncertain wanderings and countermarches; the minister disregarded the advice of his general, the Count of Aranda, who, being on the spot, was the best qualified to take a decided part and proper measures. All military men allowed the purity of his intentions, and his prudence, by which alone he repaired the mischiefs occasioned by the disorder in the supplies and hospitals, and enabled the army, by a restoration of health and order, to commence the following campaign under better auspices. His plan was to move against Coimbra, and also seize upon Oporto; the only way to derive any benefit from the capture of Almeida, and to make amends for the lost time. It is clear that if Aranda could have put this project in execution, the war of Portugal would have ended in a very different manner; but still the Count had discerned only a small part of the only plan capable of finishing the war of Portugal in two months, for he would have left time for the enemy to cover Lisbon, and to render the approaches extremely difficult.

After taking Almeida an army advances into Beira, and there meets with the Serra da Estrella, forming a tremendous barrier before the capital. Then you must expect to have to encounter an army of 20,000 Portuguese, and 7000 British soldiers: what is to be done against such a force, entrenched among the mountains, where there is no passage for waggons and artillery, especially if you are without maps, scouts, light baggage, medicines, and provisions, harassed and surrounded by 30,000 brave and desperate peasants.

CHAPTER V.

ESTREMADURA.

PORTUGUESE Estremadura is bounded north by Beira; east and south by Alemtejo; west by the Ocean: is one hundred and twenty miles long, and seventy wide; divided from east to west by the Tagus, which falls into the sea a little below Lisbon. Its soil the best in Portugal, produces all its different sorts of fruit; its commerce very considerable, carried on, in great part, by the Brazil fleet. It contains two cities, 111 towns, and 660,000 inhabitants, comprised in six corregedorias, two ouvidorias, and 460 parishes, exclusive of the country of Setuval, which contains a corregedoria and two ouvidorias.

The corregedoria of Lisbon comprises only that metropolis and its district, but reckons 360,000 inhabitants.

Lisbon is situated like an amphitheatre along the Tagus, upon seven high hills and intermediate eminences. If you take in the suburbs, its length reaches near four miles, by two in width. Its latitude 38° 42' 50"; its longitude 9° 3'. According to the fables of antiquaries, it was built 278 years after the flood, by a grandson of Noah, called Elisa; then rebuilt by Ulysses, who gave it the name of Ulyssipona*, which is still its appellation in Latin. It was a municipium under the Romans; and at present is the seat of a patriarch, first instituted in 1708. Its college of canons, who are all dignified with the title of Monsignore, and are chosen from the first families

---

* This name is a geographical barbarism; the Latin name of Lisbon is variously written, *Ulysippo*, *Olyssippo*, and *Olysippo*; the true spelling ought to be *Olisipo*. T.

of the kingdom, is extremely rich. The patriarch, on solemn days and functions, dresses like the pope, and his canons like cardinals. The city is divided into two towns or sees; the western governed by the patriarch, and the eastern by an archbishop, who is however subordinate to the patriarch. The number of parishes is thirty-seven, of convents of men thirty-two, and of nuns eighteen.

The approach to Lisbon from the sea is defended by the forts of St. Julian and Bugio, which cross their fire, and command the bar: the former, which stands high, and was built during the minority of Don Sebastian, is cut out of the solid stone in an irregular style, because it was necessary to conform to the shape of the rocks, but is almost impregnable; it consists of five irregular bastions and a ravelin on the land side, other works and a number of batteries towards the river. South of this castle is the tower of Bugio, or St. Laurence, placed on a mound of rock and sand in the middle of the river, in form circular, but of small dimensions; the batteries numerous. Between these two forts runs the bar of Lisbon, crossed in the middle by a bank of stone, called Os Cachopos, which begins at the distance of a gun-shot from fort St. John, or St. Julian, and runs up above six miles to the S. S. W. The channel on the north side is called the Corredor, (or Barra Pequena) from its narrowness, and is not attempted without a leading wind and the tide. The southern channel, much wider, is called A Carreira da Alcaçova. Two miles below Lisbon rises the tower of Bellem, near the beach, where vessels are visited by the officers of the customs. Don Manoel erected it by the name of St. Vincent. To the south of it stands the tower of Velha on a rock, its batteries traversing with those of Bellem. There are some batteries level with the water, but very ill distributed. The situation of the city is extraordinary, and, from its great unevenness, little susceptible of regular embellishments. Since the earthquake, which overwhelmed thirty thousand of its inhabitants, Lisbon is little better than a heap of ruins, of tottering palaces, and burnt churches, resembling the demolition of a fortress blown up with gunpowder.

The climate is remarkably pure and salubrious, but subject to violent falls of rain, storms, and earthquakes. The streets are full of filth, and as they are all uneven, hilly, and ill paved, the only vehicles in common use are calashes, drawn by two mules. The only level space is called the Rocio, and runs along the river side about a mile and a half, being near a mile broad; here formerly stood the royal palace, overthrown to its very foundations by the earthquake; the Count d'Oeyras is covering this space once more with splendid edifices, and straight well-paved streets; it will be ornamented with a broad quay, an arsenal, and a custom-house.

The king lives at Bellem, three miles from Lisbon, encamped in wooden barracks, for he dares not sleep under a house of stone; nor is he to blame; for there have been earthquakes every year since 1755. And had it not been for the necessity of being near so fine a harbour, and the enormous expence attending a change, the whole court would have been removed to Oporto.

The port of Lisbon is indisputably one of the finest in Europe; it has a reach of two miles, sheltered from every wind, easy of access for any tonnage, and for any number of ships; nothing is wanting but a commodious quay for landing and carrying goods: vessels of all nations flock hither, and a prodigious trade is carried on by foreign merchants; most of it is in the hands of the English; and Lisbon in fact may be considered as an English factory, both on account of the number of British subjects resident here in great state and affluence, and of the influence which the court of St. James's has over the politics of that of Portugal.

The corregedoria of Torres Vedras contains 18 towns and 40,000 souls. The town was an ancient Roman præsidium, as its Latin name of Turres* Veteres denotes.

The corregedoria of Alenquer comprizes eight burghs and 28,000 inhabitants. Alenquer was built by the Alani, and reckons 2000 souls; it would be an excellent post for a corps of troops to awe or defend Lisbon.

The corregedoria of Leyria is composed of an episcopal city, 21 towns, and 60,000 inhabitants. Leyria, a bishop's see, stands in a plain near the Lis and the Lena, with a strong old castle, and 3600 inhabitants.

The corregedoria of Thomar comprehends 19 towns and 40,000 souls. Thomar was built by Don Galdim Paez, grand-master of the Knights Templars in 1145, a little after

* This is a mere translation of the Portuguese name, and there is no other ground for the conjecture of the author. T.

the institution of the order of Christ. In 1338, King Dennis and Pope John XXII. assigned to the latter order all the possessions belonging to the former, which had been destroyed in 1312. This town contains 3600 inhabitants.

The ouvidoria of Abrantes has but two burghs, and 12,000 souls. Abrantes, situated on the right shore of the Tagus, is a very ancient place. In the reign of Augustus it was already a municipium: John V. erected it into a marquisate. It may be considered as the key of the Tagus, and would soon become a considerable place, if the government were to fortify it, and encourage the navigation of the river up into the country.

The ouvidoria of Ourem is a county, belonging to the reigning branch, and reckons but seven burghs, and 10,000 souls. Ourem, on an eminence, has 1800 inhabitants.

The corregedoria of Santarem contains fifteen towns and 50,000 souls. Santarem is built in the form of a crescent upon the Tagus, about fifty miles from Lisbon, overlooking a noble plain; its walls are ancient, with six gates, and an old citadel, to which Alphonso VI. added a pitiful horn-work, without curtain or outworks. The Romans called this place Scalabis and Præsidium Julium. It has often been besieged by the Moors, and its plains have frequently been the scenes of victories obtained over them; often has it been the residence of kings, and now is very rich, containing 8000 inhabitants, and a chapter of the order of Avis.

The country of Setuval, on the left side of the Tagus, comprizes three jurisdictions; the corregedoria of Almada, the ouvidoria of Setuval, appertaining to the order of St. Jago, and the ouvidoria of Azeitao, which belonged to the house of Aveiro; there are in it 20 towns, and 20,000 souls. Setuval, which our sailors have corrupted to St. Ubes, was founded by Alphonsos, first king of Portugal, nearly opposite the site of Cætobriga, a Roman colony, on the other side of the river Caldao, where they stationed their fleet; the place is now occupied by the village of Troya. Setuval exports a great deal of salt, oil, oranges, and wine of excellent quality, the greatest part of which goes to England. The town is well built, environed with ancient walls and massy towers; but from the increase of population a second town has been formed beyond this inclosure, and this has been fortified after the modern manner by John IV. with eleven bastions, two demi-bastions, a horn-work, a fort with four bastions, and another in a pentagon form. The place is commanded by the castle of St. Philip, erected by Philip III. of Spain; in it is a numerous train of artillery, and a fine cistern. On the shore, about a mile off, is the tower of Outaō, a lighthouse joined to a small redoubt, called As Vieiras. There are 1100 inhabitants, many of them in affluent circumstances: its red wine is equal in repute to that of Oporto, and its muscadine wine is most exquisite.

The Portuguese Estremadura ought to be, in all wars, a primary object with the Spaniards; this fertile province can supply an abundance of provisions for an army, that would die of hunger in any other part of Portugal. The Tagus facilitates the carriage of stores and ammunition to Lisbon, which is the point whither Spain must tend, when she means to make peace, to indemnify herself for her losses by sea, and treat upon a perfect equality with her inveterate foes. Her own weakness even, and the fear of not succeeding in the other points of attack, ought to spirit her up to a vigorous assault on this quarter: this plan of warfare must be rapid, without baggage, and without sieges; the event of a battle is doubly hazardous for the enemy; contributions in kind would feed the army, and those imposed in specie upon Lisbon would cover the expence of the campaign; but the attack must be resolute and steady, the country well explored, and the manœuvres executed with decision and promptitude. This province, however, is susceptible of a strong defence, by reason of its great unevenness of surface, and of the multitude of good positions that may be taken to protect the capital. Villa Velha and Abrantes are known to be important posts, but the Portuguese have never yet attempted a stand there. The plain of Santarem and the heights of Alenquer may be occupied to great advantage, as a means of defence, and the campaign may be rendered bloody and indecisive by desultory engagements. Even the metropolis, though an open place, may be defended inch by inch, if the Portuguese be resolute; and its conquest may become a work of bloodshed and difficulty.

CHAPTER VI.

ALEMTEJO.

THE province of Alemtejo borders to the north upon the Portuguese Estremadura and part of Beira; to the east upon Spanish Estremadura; to the south upon the Algarve; and to the west upon the Atlantic and part of Portuguese Estremadura. It is one hundred and forty miles long, by eighty wide. Its soil varies greatly as to its productions; in some parts it is surprisingly fruitful, and in others mountainous, sandy, or burnt up and desert. The climate very unhealthy, especially in summer, on account of the vast quantity of stagnant waters, and the want of springs and rivers. Its greatest products are corn, wine, lemons, citrons, and oranges; it has quarries of fine stone, and many sorts of rich marbles, such as the white of Estremoz, the green of Borba and Villa Viçosa, the red and white of Setuval and Arabida; the clays of Montemor o Novo and Estremoz, much employed in pottery ware. It is quite covered with fortified places, and has always been the theatre of war when the Castilians have invaded Portugal, and frequently the scene of their defeats. It contains four cities, upwards of 100 burghs, and about 280,000 inhabitants; of which the archbishoprick of Evora possesses 215,000, the bishoprick of Elvas 40,000, and the bishoprick of Portalegre 25,000. It is divided into eight jurisdictions.

The corregedoria of Evora contains one city and twelve burghs. It is a place of great antiquity, and was the abode of the famous Viriatus and Sertorius, the latter of whom added towers to its walls, and caused its celebrated aqueduct to be erected, called *Agoa da Prata*. John III. made it the place of his residence, and strengthened it with modern fortifications. It is surrounded with twelve bastions and two demi-bastions; to the north it has also a square fort, composed of four bastions and as many ravelins, through which passes the aqueduct of Sertorius. The archbishop of Evora, Don de Saldanha, is the chief judge of the kingdom, whose revenues exceed 200,000 crusades per annum. This city, which contains 12,000 inhabitants, was taken by Don Juan of Austria, son of Philip III. in 1663, and retaken by the Portuguese, who defeated that general at Ameixal. Estremoz is the residence of the governor of Alemtejo; it is a very pretty town, situate in a very fertile country: it is surrounded by ten bastions, three demi-bastions, several ravelins, and a covered way. The castl is very ancient, but it has been strengthened by four bastions and two demi-bastions; it is, however, commanded on the south by an hill, upon which a square fort, called Saint Joseph, has been constructed, with four bastions and a ravelin, covered by a tenaille towards the country. To the north there is another height at a considerable distance from the place, defended by a redoubt, called Santa Barbara. Nevertheless, with all this appearance of strength, Estremoz is incapable of defence, from the ancient, decayed, and ill-constructed state of its fortifications. It contains near 10,000 inhabitants.

The ouvidoria of Beja comprehends a city, and three towns or burghs; it is situate about nine miles from Evora, and about two from the Guadiana, in a fertile and cheerful country. Julius Cæsar gave it the name of *Pax Julia;* it contains 5000 inhabitants. Moura is within a short mile of the Guadiana: its fortifications were demolished by the Spaniards in the war of the succession, and they have since received little or no reparations, particularly the castle.

The ouvidoria of Campo do Ourique contains fifteen burghs. Ourique is remarkable for little else than the victory which Alphonso Henriquez, first king of Portugal, obtained over five Moorish kings or governors. His army consisted of no more than three thousand men, by whom, and the revelations of an inspired crucifix, he was proclaimed king on the field of battle. It belongs to the order of St. James.

The ouvidoria of Villa Viçosa belongs to the house of Bragança, and contains twelve burghs; Villa Viçosa is nineteen miles to the west of Elvas, and situate in a very fertile plain: it is but indifferently fortified, though famous for a battle gained by the Marquis of Marialva and the Count of Schomberg, against the Marquis of Caracene, in which the Spaniards lost 15,000 men. Here is a fine palace, and a beautiful park stocked with deer, belonging to the Bragança family.

The corregedoria of Elvas consists of an episcopal city and six burghs. Elvas is situate fourteen miles to the west of Badajoz. Though its position is elevated, it is commanded by several heights, of which the two nearest to the town have been fortified. Its origin is attributed to the Gauls, about the year of the world 3009. The fortifications are not very important; they consist of four royal bastions, as many demi-bastions, and a redan. On its south side is fort La Lippe, which the General of that name began in 1763, and whose works are nearly finished: it is not well calculated to defend the place, and demands a very strong garrison. Here is a very beautiful aqueduct, the maintenance of which is attended with great expence. This town was besieged in 1658, by Don Louis de Haro; but the Count Cantanhede came to its relief, forced the lines of the Castilians, killed 6000 of their men, and took 1000 prisoners; with their artillery, ammunition, and baggage.

Olivença is situate on the left side of the Guadiana. Its situation, seven miles from the river, is pleasant, particularly that of the castle; it is very populous, and contains near 5000 inhabitants. Campo Mayor, situate opposite to Alburquerque and Badajoz, is a place of considerable importance to this province. Count Schomberg, the saviour of Portugal, strengthened this place with a well-constructed fort; but the fortifications, and a part of the town, were destroyed 16th September, 1732, by the blowing up of a powder magazine; which unfortunate event has greatly weakened as well as dispeopled the place, though the works have been in some measure repaired. At the close of the campaign of 1762, the Spaniards, in order to retrieve their reputation, ordered a considerable detachment to take Campo Mayor; but General Don Gregorio de Muniara, the present minister of war, who commanded that expedition, having failed in arriving before it till it was broad daylight, did not think proper to hazard an attack, and retired without attempting any thing.

The corregedoria of Portalegre consists of one episcopal city, and twelve burghs. Portalegre is situate on a gentle elevation, fifteen miles from Spain: its fortifications are ancient and incapable of defence. It contains between 5 and 6000 inhabitants. Arronches is between Portalegre and Campo Mayor, at an equal distance from them both. It owes its foundation to the first kings of Portugal, and is fortified in the ancient manner.

The ouvidoria of Crato contains twelve burghs. Crato belongs to a priory of the order of Malta, and is inclosed by walls.

The ouvidoria of Avis is composed of seventeen burghs. The town is situated on a river of the same name, and forms a triangle with Arayolos and Estremoz. It is the principal place of the order of Avis, which was first founded at Evora: it has but few inhabitants, and is surrounded with ancient walls. Its territory extends several miles, and belongs to the order.

Alemtejo has been the perpetual theatre of triumph to the Portuguese, and defeat to the Spaniards; nor could it be otherwise. The Spaniards formerly maintained the ill-founded opinion that Alemtejo offered a passage to Lisbon, because it is the post-road. The Tagus, furnished with an army to oppose the passage, cannot be crossed; an army which enters Alemtejo cannot extend its hostilities beyond that province, or at most to Algarve. But the conquest of them both would effect nothing of importance, and can never give a shock to the Portuguese monarchy, whose strength is to be found in Lisbon, Oporto, and America. The strong places of Alemtejo are not in a state to make any vigorous defence; but, besides the expence employed and time lost in taking them, the climate is so fatal, that an army, in spite of every precaution, and the utmost exertions of medical assistance, must necessarily fall a prey to hunger, thirst, and epidemic diseases. The Portuguese cannot wish for a more fortunate circumstance, in a war with Spain, than that their enemies may commence and push on their operations in this province.

CHAPTER VII.

ALGARVE.

THE kingdom of Algarve is bounded on the north by the province of Alemtejo; on the east it borders on Andalusia; and to the south and west is terminated by the sea. Its length is about ninety miles, and its breadth from twenty to twenty-five. It was conquered by Sancho II. and has since belonged to the crown of Portugal, notwithstanding the ill-founded claims of Spain. It was afterwards retaken by the Moors, but Alphonso III. reunited it altogether to his dominions, by the capture of Faro. The length of coast from Cape St. Vincent to Almeria, with the opposite shores of Africa, comprising Ceuta and Tangier, then in the possession of the kings of Portugal, were named Algarve;* and on this account the sovereigns of Portugal have preserved the title of King of Algarve on this side, and beyond the sea in Africa. This small country possesses an uncommon degree of fertility, and is capable of nourishing four times the number of its present inhabitants. It produces grain, wine, oil, and abundance of fruits, as figs, grapes, and sweet almonds, in which it carries on a considerable trade. The tunny fishery has been more extensive than it is at present, but it still continues to form a principal revenue of this kingdom. It contains four cities, twelve burghs, sixty villages, and 65,000 inhabitants, divided into two corregedorias, and one ouvidoria.

The corregedoria of Lagos comprehends seven burghs and one city. Lagos is situated on the south-east shore of Algarve, at twenty-four miles from cape Saint Vincent. Its bay is secure from winds at N. N. E. and is capable of receiving the largest ships (though it is not without

* They are called so to this day, being the extremity of that part of Africa named by the Arabs *al Garb*, or the West. T.

rocks), and the entrance is protected by a battery of cannon. Twenty miles of the coast from Lagos to Sagres are defended by five forts. This town was first built by the Carthaginians: it is fortified in an irregular manner, but possesses a good citadel called Pinhao, which is the residence of the governors and captains general of this kingdom. Lagos contains 2800 inhabitants. Villa Nova de Portimao is nine miles to the east of Lagos, and is seated on a river which forms a spacious and secure harbour, above a mile broad, and three fathoms deep; but the entrance is dangerous, and requires the assistance of a pilot. This river is navigable to Sylves, with boats only, though it is at no greater distance than eight miles. Each side of the bar is defended by a fort: on the west is that called St. Catherine's, and on the east is St. John's. These two towns contain together about 4000 souls.

The corregedoria of Tavira comprises a city and three burghs. Tavira is seated on a bay of the same name, about seventeen miles from Faro, and fifteen from Ayamonte, a frontier town of Andalusia. The bar is low and irregular, and the channel at the entrance is five fathoms deep. The harbour is protected by two forts, and the place contains about 5000 inhabitants. It is divided into two towns by the river Sequa, over which there is a fine stone bridge. Loule is a small town eight miles N. by W. of Faro, of an ancient appearance, and contains upwards of 4000 souls. Alcoutim is situated at sixteen miles from Castromarim, opposite San Lucar de Guadiana, and contains only 1000 inhabitants. It is the last town in Algarve on the side of Andalusia.

The ouvidoria of Faro comprehends two cities, of which one is episcopal, a single burgh, and a few villages. Faro is distant seventeen miles from Tavira, and thirteen from the fortress of Quarteira, which defends the coast. Its bar is narrow and variable. Its fortifications are modern, but were very much injured by the last earthquake, which made great devastation in Algarve. The bishopric of Sylves was transferred to Faro in 1580, and the town itself was burned in 1596 by the English.* It contains at present 7600 inhabitants, and possesses a considerable trade, many foreign merchants being

* It had been plundered first, and the library of the famous bishop Osovio, or the greatest part of it, became the share of the Earl of Essex, who gave it to the university of Oxford. T.

established there. Three times every month a packet-boat arrives there from Gibraltar, for the benefit of the English. At about three miles north between Faro and Loule, there is a village called Estoy, built on the ruins of the ancient Ossobona.*

The kingdom of Algarve is almost impenetrable to the Spaniards; nor indeed would an entrance into it be attended with any advantage. In the various wars, therefore, between the two nations it has remained undisturbed, holding forth to the invader no other temptation but internal wretchedness. Its sea coast might be invaded, and its tunny fishery ruined; but, in general, the inhabitants of Cadiz and the coast of Andalusia have, in that respect, more to lose than to gain. The coast might be made to furnish good seamen, if the government encouraged such a design. But, after all, this province is of little importance or utility to the Portuguese monarchy, though it is dignified with the pompous title of a kingdom.

* Read Ossonoba.

CHAPTER VIII.

CONCLUSION.

I might have extended these geographical details, which I have in a great measure extracted from the best authors, and which have been confirmed by such inhabitants of the different provinces as were qualified to instruct me; but I leave history to historians, local description to geographers, and wander not beyond the limits which I have prescribed to myself. The curious will find nothing to satisfy them on the subject of natural history; I have given the whole of my attention to matters of the most interesting nature, because it flatters, more than any other, the pride, the ambition, and the more furious passions of men, I mean the science of attack and defence. For war, that indispensable scourge, demands the study of almost all the branches of human knowledge, and the application of them to one object.

The ignorance and want of skill which the Spaniards have displayed in their attacks on Portugal; and the Portuguese have manifested in their defence of it, present examples of military exertion, which alternately call forth our ridicule or compassion. At the same time, they prove, without a possibility of contradiction, that these countries, in the art of war, are at least two or three centuries behind the rest of Europe.

Portugal has acquired a great share of consideration in the affairs of Europe. Several of its powers are connected with this kingdom, by the interests of commerce, and the bonds of alliance. When the chances of war left the political balance of Europe in a perfect equilibrium, these connections and relations did not require particular examination; but at present it is indispensably necessary to obtain a clear view of them. They, however, explain each other, and proceed from the events of past, as they depend upon those of future wars.

It is in this point of view alone, that I wish to unfold the situation of Portugal, that my countrymen, who may hereafter be employed in any affairs that may relate to this kingdom, hitherto so little known, may be qualified with such information as will be useful to them.

Spain alone is worse peopled than Portugal. Throughout the whole peninsula nature appears in its original and uncultivated state. The plains of Alemtejo from Ourique to Almada, and those of Beira, from Lisbon, Leyria, and Coimbra, to Oporto, are abandoned to themselves by the sluggishness of their inhabitants, and are become sandy, burnt up, and pestilential.

Portugal is uncommonly well watered, and contains upwards of an hundred and twenty rivers, great and small, which traverse it in all directions. Nevertheless the province of Entre Douro e Minho alone seems to derive any considerable advantage from them. Alemtejo, with more than thirty rivers, and numerous springs, possesses a parched and barren soil, while the marshes and stagnant waters which the inhabitants never attempt to drain, are the perpetual cause of fevers, of pestilence, of famine, and of death. Poverty is the least of those evils, which the Portuguese prefer to labour: with little more than can just sustain nature, they crawl and languish through life in filth, in pain, in ignorance, and superstition. Their base and sluggish natures subject them to want, to pain, and disease, in the finest country in the world, and which would be the most wholesome and the happiest, if it were better peopled.

I except, nevertheless, from this representation, which is but too true, the Entre Douro e Minho, a part of Traz os Montes; some small portions of Beira, the right bank of the Tagus, the territory of Lisbon, with those of Setuval, Estremoz, Elvas, and Faro. The population of this kingdom is supposed to be as follows:

Provinces.	Inhabitants.
Entre Douro e Minho	504,000
Traz os Montes	156,000
Beira	560,000
Estremadura	660,000
Alemtejo	280,000
Algarve	65,000
Total	2,225,000

This is a very large number of inhabitants, when compared with the population of Spain, but by no means proportioned to the extent, the fertility, and the climate of Portugal; and it would require an age of successive administrations equal to that of Count d'Oeyras, to place this kingdom in a state of power, strength, cultivation, and populousness, of which it is susceptible, and of which the negligent and supine disposition of its inhabitants has hitherto deprived it.

BOOK II.

THE PORTUGUESE COLONIES.

CHAPTER I.

DIVISION.

The Portuguese colonies were first acquired by force, and without difficulty, and the greater part have been lost in the same manner. The revolutions which have deprived the kingdom of Portugal of a part of its establishments, were the natural result of the weak condition in which the Portuguese power remained, after the catastrophe of its sovereign, Don Sebastian, and its subjection to Spain; they did not even want to be precipitated by the irruption of other nations of Europe, which have so easily overthrown, in every quarter of the globe, the precarious power and exaggerated glory of the Portuguese.

To facilitate the consideration of the subject before us, I shall divide the Portuguese colonies into four chapters, under the titles of Asia, Africa, America, and the Portuguese islands. More extensive information may be acquired of them in the following works: Decades of the Indies, by J. de Barros; the Chronology of America, by P. Sim. Vasconcelos; Memoirs of Pernambucco, of Duarte, Albuquerque, Coelho, and the war of Brasil, by J. de Sta Theresa; America Portuguesa de Rocha de Pitta: though none of these authors have been translated. The history of Congo, by P. Labat; the history of Brasil, and the general history of Voyages, may also be consulted.

CHAPTER II.

ASIA.

This quarter of the globe is the ancient and most distinguished theatre of the glory of the Portuguese, and consequently the present and future monument of their shame and downfall: they were the first conquerors of the East Indies; of which, for near a century, they remained the sole possessors, and their language still continues to be the commercial language of the settlements which have long since ceased to be under their dominion; but when the other European nations, and particularly the Dutch, penetrated into these distant seas, the Portuguese were driven from their settlements with the same ease as they had acquired them.

The Portuguese historians, with the exaggerating spirit of their country, have given strange and incredible accounts of their Oriental conquests. Such are the incomprehensible sieges of Diu and Ormuz, of Malacca and Goa. Nevertheless, it cannot be denied, that during a century they were absolute masters of the sea and its coasts, from the Red sea and the Persian gulf, to China, Japan, and the islands of Liqueo. So vast an empire, in the hands of a nation so feeble, must necessarily fall of itself, while it occasioned a very great depopulation of the mother country. It is indeed a question of no certain determination whether the Portuguese have lost or gained by the diminution of their colonies.

At present this immense empire, far more extensive than the conquests, and even than the ideas of Alexander the Great, is reduced to the town of Goa, and certain factories; as those of Chaul, Daman, Baçaim (Basseen), and the island of Macao, in China. These establishments are in the most miserable condition, and possess a very small share of commercial importance. One ship alone sails from Lisbon to the East Indies in a year, and this vessel, so far from adding to the royal revenues, costs the king upwards of 200,000 crusades.* The trade between China and Portugal is carried on by the English, who, from their superior skill and active character, make the voyage in half the time required by the Portuguese, who have ever been very indifferent navigators; a circumstance

* About £10,000.

which must be an invincible obstacle to the progress of their East Indian commerce. But to give a conclusive idea of the condition of the Portuguese colonies in Asia, or the East Indies, it is only necessary to add, that there is not more than 4500 Portuguese established in the five towns already named; that the Asiatic colonies are a burden to Portugal, that they draw from it its specie, and return a losing trade. That, after all, the king continues to maintain them from no other motives but a certain political necessity, and national pride.

The clearest revenue of the king arises from the confiscation he makes every three years of the property and effects of the viceroys, and other public officers, who return from the Indies. They all undergo a process, and generally a criminal one, as soon as they arrive from thence, are sent to prison, and think themselves very happy if they preserve their lives, and escape the horrors of perpetual imprisonment at the expence of their ill-acquired fortune. When the Portuguese fidalgos determine to go to India, they instantly forget every idea of duty and honour; they banish all sense of shame, deliver themselves up to the most rapacious avarice; they no longer are sensible either of virtue or remorse; they rule by extortion and all means are the same to them that procure them wealth. Hence it is, that the commerce of the Indies has altogether declined; and how is it possible that it should exist, when instead of that protection and justice which it ought to receive from the persons employed by the king, it meets with nothing but vexation, venality, artifice, and tyranny. The king receives, at least, 5 or 600,000 crusades from the confiscations of each viceroy every three years. But though crimes are punished, the people are not avenged; at the same time commerce is ruined, and the king gains some present advantages by exhausting the sources of them.

It has been proposed to sell the five Oriental settlements, already mentioned, to the English or the Dutch; but they are not objects of acquisition to either of those nations. The port of Goa is very inconvenient, the bar that crosses it is extremely dangerous, and its territory is unhealthy. Chaul, Baçaim, and Daman are but small places, in bad situations, and all of them on the eastern coast of the Peninsula,

' 25,000 or 30,000.

on this side of the Ganges, where those two powers are already in possession of more commodious establishments. The Dutch are masters of the whole coast by Calecut, Cochin, Cranganore, Cananore, upon the coast of Malabar; Onore, Barcelore, and Mangalore, on the coast of Canara, and Vingorla, between Goa and Chaul, all of which they took from the Portuguese. The English have no other settlement in this part of India but Bombay, which they bought of the Portuguese, and which is sufficient for them as a depot for their trade, with Surat, Ormuz, and the Red Sea. Besides, the course of trade has been transferred from the eastern to the western side of the Peninsula, and the commerce of the Indies is absorbed by the English Company, established at Bengal and Madras.

CHAPTER III.

AFRICA.

THE Portuguese maintain a greater degree of power in this part of the globe; nevertheless it is not sufficient to prevent their commerce from declining. Indeed this commerce is almost entirely annihilated, since the English, French, Dutch, and Danes, have established themselves along the coast of Guinea; and particularly since the Dutch have formed the superb settlement of the Cape of Good Hope. The Portuguese colonies in Africa formerly extended from Tangier and Ceuta to the Red Sea. A few factories on the coast of Guinea, and that of Malagueta (or Grain coast), all of which are in a wretched condition; the kingdom of Congo, some small forts in the Monomotapa, Quilimane, Quiloa, Melinde, Monbaça, Brava, and Moçambique, which is the residence of a governor-general, are all that remain in subjection to Portugal. The only interesting part of these colonies is the kingdom of Congo. This country has been made known by the general history of voyages, and a particular history of P. Labat. The general residence of the Portuguese governor is Saint Paul de Loanda, a large and populous town, which contains 5000 white inhabitants, and 50,000 slaves or negroes.

The king of Congo is under the protection of the sovereign of Portugal, to whom, though an independent prince, he pays a tribute. There are also six princes who are tributary to him, who are continually engaged in war against him, or with each other. These divisions are fomented by the Portuguese, in order to purchase the captives of either party. The Catholic religion has made a considerable progress in this country, but blended with Pagan superstitions. The natives are so wicked and perfidious that the Portuguese have not been able to form any establishments in the interior parts of the country. They have a fort 30 leagues from the coast, called Massengano, erected for the purpose of preventing the barbarous nations of Caffreria from making irruptions into the kingdoms of Congo and Angola. The Dutch possessed themselves of the kingdom of Benguela, which was a part of the viceroyalty of Congo; (but it belongs now to the Portuguese and its capital, St. Philip de Benguela, is a very trading town). All these forts are peopled and defended by criminals condemned in Portugal to perpetual imprisonment. The commerce of Congo is in slaves, copper, white pepper, (ivory), and sugar. But after all, the possessions in Africa are rather a matter of honour than of gain to the king of Portugal. Though there are not less than fifteen African princes who are tributary to his crown, he does not receive a million of crusades* from the joint produce of their tribute, and the languishing commerce which is carried on by his subjects with their country: while his forts, &c. though they are ill kept up, and worse provided, cost him more than he receives. Hence it is, that the greater part of these establishments are considered merely as prisons, to which malefactors, nobles, and disgraced ministers are exiled; particularly those of Massengano, in the kingdom of Angola, and Mazagan, (on the coast of Morocco). In the latter of these, the minister Diego de Mendoça, the predecessor of Count d'Oeyras, finished his career, after having been reduced to gain his bread by teaching in a school, as Dionysius the tyrant had done before him.

* About £50,000.

CHAPTER IV.

AMERICA.

The most valuable colony possessed by Portugal is that of Brasil. This country merits a very particular description, and from its situation and character may have some influence on the wars carried on by the different sovereigns of Europe, as well as in the negotiations of the cabinets of Versailles, of London, of Madrid, and Lisbon.

Brasil is above 600 great leagues in length, from north to south, and near 700 in breadth, from east to west. It is bounded to the north by the river of Amazons and Guiana; to the east by the sea; to the south by the river La Plata; and to the west by the country of Amazons, (Peru, and several intermediary nations). It has 1200 leagues of coast, and is inhabited in certain places, and on the banks of certain rivers, to the distance of 400 leagues up the interior of the country. But the principal settlements of the Portuguese do not extend more than 50 leagues from the coast, on account of the savages; who have been so cruelly treated by the European invaders as to become their irreconcileable enemies. But, however the Portuguese may misrepresent the natives, they are in themselves an honest, honourable, and inoffensive people. We have the authority of the Jesuits for this character, who instructed them in the nature and duties of civil society, and formed them into the wise republic of Paraguay; which is as disgraceful to the Portuguese and the Spaniards, as it is honourable to humanity, to the Jesuits, and the savages themselves.

Brasil is divided into fourteen provinces, according to the following arrangement; proceeding from north to south.

1. The capitania or province of Para occupies the northern boundary of Brasil. Its capital is named Nossa Senhora de Belem, (more properly Para) it is a bishopric, situated on the great river of Amazons, and is defended by a strong citadel, as well as a fort, called Nossa Senhora das Merces, at the mouth of the river Muju, which forms the port of Para. It is guarded by four companies of soldiers, and the number of troops in this province amount to about 800 men. This town contains from 8 to 10,000 inhabitants; its port is capable of receiving

vessels of a large tonnage, and there is a particular company established for carrying on the commerce of this province, and that of Maranham. This company, however, is in a very declining state, because, on account of the duties that the directors have imposed on European commodities, and to which the colonists are obliged to submit, these two provinces owe more to the company than the country is worth. The Count d'Oeyras is at the head of this commercial corporation, and the most deeply interested in its success. He it is, therefore, that supports this ill-conceived right of imposing duties which he obtained for, or rather granted to, this company.

The principal commodities which are exported from Para are sugar, which is manufactured at upwards of thirty sugar-works in the interior part of the country, coffee, vanilla, cloves, sarsaparilla, and Brasil wood, particularly that beautiful species of it called Burapemina; and the Umiri, whose trunk distils an odoriferous oil, and whose bark, when burnt, scents as a perfume. At the distance of four leagues from Para, in passing down the river of Amazons, there is a tongue of land divided into several islands, the largest of which is that called

Joannes; it is very populous, and defended by several forts. These islands belong to different Portuguese fidalgos, with the title of baronies. About a league and an half from the town is the burgh of St. George dos Alamos, with a regular fortress. At the distance of forty leagues from the mouth, and on the bank of the river, is another burgh, called Camuta, with the fort of Curupa. Along the river is the fort of Paru, which the French took and demolished in 1698, and those of Tapajos and Rio Negro. The province of Para is terminated to the north by Cayenne, or French Guyana. Its boundary on this side is the North Cape, with the fort of Macapa, opposite that of Comau, and the fort of Aragoariz. In this province there are four towns or burghs; Para, St. George dos Alamos, Camuta, and Cahete, with about 50,000 inhabitants. The government of Para depends upon that of Maranham.

The Portuguese have lately formed establishments on the Rio Negro, where they have discovered some new mines of gold and diamonds. In the year 1766, 400 marine soldiers, workmen in every branch, and several families, were sent out from Lisbon, with many peculiar privileges, to this settlement: but in time of war it is very much exposed to the incursions of the French, as it is in the neighbourhood their new settlements in Guiana; and at a great distance from any succour that could be afforded it from Bahia, or even from Para and Maranham.

This new colony of Rio Negro has been very injudiciously conducted by Francis Xavier de Mendoça, minister of the marine department. The unhappy colonists not only were refused those advantages which were necessary for their success, but were deceived in the agreements originally entered into with them, respecting their settlement. This colony was, indeed, reinforced by those French families who were obliged to abandon Guiana, after the failure of those establishments which had been formed along the river Courou.

2. The province of Maranham, is by no means well peopled, but in the island of St. Louis, which contains about 15,000 inhabitants. This island is twenty-six leagues in circumference, and is very fertile. The town which is called St. Louis is a bishopric, defended by a citadel and several forts, and has a very commodious harbour. It is the residence

of the governor-general of the three northern provinces.

3. The province of Seara, has but one small fort, that defends the harbour of Seara, which is capable only of receiving boats. It has very little commerce, and does not contain more than 10,000 souls.

These three provinces, which would greatly aggrandize the French in this part of the globe, might be very easily conquered; they are rich and fertile, and contain 80,000 inhabitants, of which the Portuguese do not form a sixth part. This is a very predominant motive to induce France to encourage and support the settlement of Guiana, which lies at the back of them. If the French should take the opportunity of any future war to fall upon these three provinces, they would be easily subdued, as they are without the means of defence; the forts being old and in bad condition, and the troops ill disciplined. Instead of losing their time and wasting their money in founding a colony upon the river Courou, they would find, at the Rio Negro, mines already formed. Besides, by the communications there are between Para and the mines of St. Paul, they would become masters of all the riches of Brasil. Such a vigorous operation would change the whole system of these colonies, and influence the interests of Europe.

4. The capitania of Rio Grande. Cidade Nova, or Rio Grande do Norte, is the name of its capital, situate about twelve miles from the entrance of the river, which is defended by the fort Dos Reyes Magos, one of the strongest in all Brasil. The river flows from a lake between thirty and forty miles in circumference, in which are found the finest Brasil pearls.* This capitania has two towns, Parantuba, which is fortified to preserve it from the attacks of the Indians, and Cunhao. It contains about 12,000 inhabitants.

5. The province of Paraiba had been given by King John III. to the celebrated John de Barros, author of the Decades of the Indies, the Livy of Portugal, and one of the best writers in Europe; but he was obliged to restore it to the king, after he had almost ruined himself by unsuccessful armaments. The capital is Paraiba do Norte, or Nossa Senhora das

* The river is called Potiji by the Indians, and takes its source in the Aracuyas mountains; but the existence of the lake is not so well ascertained. T.

E

Neves, seated on the river Paraiba, at whose mouth there is an harbour and a custom-house, defended by a pentagonal fort, called St. Catherina. This province produces the best sugar, which is fabricated in twenty-one sugar-works. The town contains about 4000, and the province about 20,000 inhabitants.

6. The capitania of Itamaraca consists of the island of that name, and of eight or nine leagues of the coast. The town in the island is named Nossa Senhora da Conceiçaō, (our Lady of the Conception), and is situated on a hill. The island also possesses three sugar-works. Upon the main land is the town of St. Miguel de Goyana, with three parishes in its environs. This province contains about 10,000 souls.

7. The province of Pernambuco has about eighty leagues of coast. Its capital is Olinda, built in an elevated situation on the sea side; it lies in a delicious country, and is adorned with fountains. It is inhabited by about 12,000 people, and with two battalions of troops as a garrison; though one occupies the town of Recife. Olinda possesses an excellent manufactory of sword blades. The Dutch were masters of this province from the year 1624 to

1654, when they were driven out by the inhabitants. The Count Mauritius of Nassau had very much embellished the two towns of Olinda and Recife, where he built a very handsome castle. These two places have a commodious harbour defended by several forts.

Pernambuco has been a very rich province. It once possessed upwards of one hundred sugar-works, fine forests, well cultivated farms, and abundance of fruit. It then furnished upwards of 15,000 casks of sugar at every return of the Lisbon fleet; but at present it scarce produces only a fifth part. Its bishopric has a very extensive jurisdiction, and it still contains from 50 to 60,000 souls. The people, however, frequently quit it for Paraguay, Chili, and Peru, on account of the misery which is produced by the vexatious impositions of the trading companies, and the debts with which the province is burdened. It has also seven other towns, named Igaraes, Velho, Porto Calvo, Lagoa do Norte, Santo Antonio Grande, Lagoa do Sul, and Penedo on the river St. Francisco, which terminates this province on the south, as the isle of Itamaraca forms its termination to the north.

8. The capitania of Sergipe contains about

20,000 souls, with 25 sugar-works, and produces tobacco, leather, and cattle.* Besides its capital, which is called Sergipe del Rey, it has several other towns, of which the most considerable are St. Christovao, Santo Amaro das Brotas, and Villa Real do Piagui. It has no harbour sufficient to receive large vessels, which is a great obstruction to its commerce.

9. The principal capitania of Brasil is that of Bahia de Todos os Santos, (the Bay of All Saints) which is the residence of the viceroy. St. Salvador, which is the capital, is well fortified, both by sea and land, and contains a garrison of 2 or 3000 men. It has a very fine archiepiscopal palace, a very rich cathedral, and a very good harbour on the bay, from whence the province derives its name. St. Salvador is a very opulent and commercial place; and being the general rendezvous of all the fleets, it is the mart of the various commodities of Europe. This town contains above 20,000 inhabitants, and the province upwards of 100,000.

10. The capitania of Ilheos has for its capital the town of St. George, defended, as well

* It has also gold mines. T.

as its harbour, by two forts. The other places in its district are Cairu and Camanu,* whose bar is defended by a fort, consisting of four bastions. It contains above 20,000 inhabitants, is very wealthy, and its principal commerce is in meal of different kinds, with which it furnishes Bahia and Brasil.

11. The capitania or province of Porto Seguro has two towns, the chief of which bears its name, from the security of its haven; while the other is called St. Antonio on the river Caravelas. These towns and their environs contain from 7 to 8000 inhabitants.

12. The capitania of Espíritu-Santo stretches along fifty-five leagues of coast. It comprehends the towns of Spiritu-Santo, with a tolerable harbour, Os Reys Magos, Villa Ilha, and Goropari. It contains about 25,000 souls.

13. The province or capitania of Rio Janeiro. Its capital is called St. Sebastian, and is an episcopal see. The plan of it, and an account of its capture, may be seen in the Memoirs of Du Guay-Trouyn.† This province

---

* Camamu, not Camanu, belongs to the capitania of the Bay. T.

† The city of St. Sebastian is better known by the name of Rio de Janeiro, commonly Rio Janeiro,

contains upwards of 100 sugar-works. Its commerce was carried on till January 1, 1766, by a company, which the Portuguese government, for political reasons, has dissolved. It contains upwards of 40,000 inhabitants: the town of Cabo Frio, about twenty-two leagues eastward of Rio Janeiro, is opulent, from its trade in salt.

14. The capitania of St. Vincent is one of the four governments dependent on Bahia; its capital bears the same name, and contains about 3000 souls. The principal commerce of this province consists in cattle, particularly in hogs, in brandy, and sugar: it has also several forts. The dismembered government of the mines of Rio Janeiro contains ten towns or burghs, of which the capital is Santos, that contains upwards of 8000 inhabitants. I have never been able to obtain any satisfactory information respecting the produce of these mines; but it is reasonable to suppose that it has greatly diminished, from the eagerness with which those of

(River January), is at present the metropolis of Brasil, and has been for some time the residence of a viceroy. Its harbour is one of the finest in the world, and the entrance, not a mile broad, is defended by the strong forts of Santa Cruz, and Lozia, or St. John. T.

Rio Negro are worked; these have been but lately discovered, and are in a situation much more exposed to invasion. The government of St. Paul contains thirteen burghs. St. Paul is built on the famous mountain of Paranam-piacaba which possesses a most valuable mine of diamonds. Indeed, the whole of the country is rich, and in a state of cultivation. The nations who occupy the space between this province and the Rio de la Plata, or river Plate, are the Tapuyas and the Carijos, and other warlike Indians. The Tapuyas, or Tapes, form one of the principal nations of South America, and are consequently the most hostile to the Spaniards and Portuguese. This country is terminated, on the river Plate, by the colony of St. Sacrement, which is called the province of the king, and was ceded by the Spaniards at the peace of Utrecht. It consists only of that town, and sixty leagues of the bank of the river opposite Buenos Ayres. The river La Plata, from its mouth to this town, is divided (by the sand banks) into three navigable channels, viz. St. Lucia, La Conception, and El Rosario. Before this town is the island of St. Gabriel, with a castle, very necessary to protect the navigation of the river;

it was attacked and taken in 1762 and 1763, by Cevallos, commandant of the Spanish colony of Uruguay. The Portuguese in vain endeavoured to retake it: for that purpose they had taken in their pay four English privateers, but dissensions arose in this little fleet, and two of the vessels having been destroyed by fire, with all their equipage, the governor of Rio Janeiro, Gomez Freire, an officer of merit, who conducted this enterprize, was forced to abandon it, and the Portuguese did not repossess the island of St. Gabriel and the colony, till the peace. The town is very ill fortified, though so often besieged and taken by the Spaniards. It contains about 2500 inhabitants, including blacks and slaves. These four governments are so populous, that Don Pedro d'Acunha, the present viceroy of Brasil, was enabled to levy, in 1766, 14,000 militia; which measure, united to other causes, occasioned a great revolt in the mines. The number of their inhabitants is estimated at upwards of 100,000. The inhabitants of St. Paul and the mines are ferocious and insolent. The great distance from any sea-port renders it necessary to maintain a large body of troops, and to exercise an unremitting rigour, in order to keep them in submission.

This colony is composed of villains capable of committing every crime.* It is true, indeed, that they are the best soldiers which Brasil can furnish, but they occasion continual disquietude and embarrassment to the viceroy. Assassinations are very frequent in this part of Brasil, and crimes of every kind pass unpunished. Travellers are under the necessity of forming themselves into large caravans, in their journies from these interior provinces to the sea; and even with this precaution they encounter inconvenience and danger; for, besides the wicked disposition of the natives, who are habituated to assassination as well as robbery, the roads are infested by runaway negroes, who have formed settlements in the woods, which the Portuguese find it a matter of great difficulty to force and destroy.

The Maroon or free negroes are, throughout the European colonies, the most cruel enemies of their former masters, and will, in the course of time, produce the most material injury to the colonies themselves. The number of them in Brasil is impossible to determine with any degree of accuracy; but in the general estima-

* They are known by the name of *Paulists*. T.

tion of the Brasilians themselves, they exceed 40,000. Their settlements, which are situated in the most impenetrable parts of the woods, are fortified by palisades and deep ditches, while they are not altogether destitute of fire-arms, though their more common weapons are arrows and darts. These inclosures not only contain their huts, but their cattle, and are very populous; for, though so many of the Maroons are from time to time destroyed, their propagation is so abundant as to justify the calculation already given of their numbers in this part of South America.

All the European nations experience in their colonies the danger of these interior enemies, as well as the difficulty of extirpating them. The English have not been able to deliver their islands from them, particularly Jamaica.* The Dutch have lately been engaged in a war with them in their colony of Berbice. The island of Cuba, though very narrow, is so filled with them, that it is impossible to pass in safety in any direction but from the Havannah to St. Jago.

* This, however, has been luckily accomplished last year, by the indefatigable exertions of Lord Balcarras. T.

Between the colony of St. Sacrement and the capitania of St. Vincent, is inclosed the Rio St. Pedro, a Spanish settlement, and the island of St. Catherine, where they have a garrison. These two ports, especially that of Rio St. Pedro, will be a perpetual subject of dispute between the two nations; while the Spaniards refuse to sell, exchange, or abandon it. It is also as difficult for the Spaniards to preserve this port, as for the Portuguese to keep possession of that of St. Sacrement. It is to be presumed, therefore, that the latter would be very willing to make an exchange. But this port is of much greater importance to the Spaniards, than that of St. Sacrement is to the Portuguese, because in time of war, it secures the means of arriving at the mines, which are not more than 100 leagues distant, and are not guarded on this side: the possession, therefore, of this port must be the cause of continual alarm to the Portuguese; whereas their colony of St. Sacrement can occasion but a trifling degree of distrust to the Spaniards, as the breadth of Rio de la Plata, forms a sufficient defence to Buenos Ayres; and any attack that the Portuguese might make from this quarter must be of no comparative importance.

In the beginning of the year 1766 the Count d'Oeyras ordered an embarkation of 400 disciplined troops, with engineers and cannon for this part of Brasil. The Spanish garrison of Rio St. Pedro was in a very wretched condition. It consists only of 200 dragoons, and 400 infantry, which at this period had been diminished by the desertion of 140 men, who had passed over to the Portuguese. But there was no reason for supposing that any hostilities would take place, as the general revolt of Brasil then occupied the attention of the Portuguese minister.

Brasil, possessing as it does all the advantages of nature, ought to be the finest colony in the world; as the Portuguese have now been settled on it upwards of 260 years. But besides the ravages of the Dutch, it has been checked in its progress, as well as the rest of this monarchy, by the dominion of the Spaniards. It has even lost much of its value and importance since the epocha of the three Philips; the debts of John V. and the companies that have been established in it, with more avidity than understanding, have completed its ruin. Commerce now possesses but three principal positions in Brasil, and is absolutely annihilated in every other part of this immense country. These are Bahia, which is the centre of it; Para, to which the new discoveries of Rio Negro promise to restore a commercial vigour, as from thence the produce of the mines may be transported by the river Amazon; and lastly, Rio Janeiro, whose situation is equally convenient to the southern mines, and which serves as a port to the capitanias of Porto Seguro, Espiritu Santo, and St. Vincent.

In the colony of Brasil there are twelve cities, sixty-six burghs, and a great number of villages; an archbishopric, and four bishoprics, with about 430,000 inhabitants, of which a sixth part, at most, are Portuguese. About thirty vessels sail annually from this country to Portugal; which, one year with another, carry from 7 to 8000 casks of sugar, 10,000 rolls of tobacco; from 25 to 30,000 dressed hides, from 4 to 5000 raw hides, with large quantities of diamonds, as well as gold in dust, ingots, and coin; besides balm, cloves, cinnamon, ginger, cocoa, vanilla, cotton, indigo, oil of copahu, and several kinds of wood, in great estimation for their strength, length, and durability. Every year one or two frigates sail from Bahia and Fernambuco, laden with timbers already prepared for the service of the king's marine. The negroes employed in this colony are brought from Ethiopia* and Congo. Neither the king of Portugal, or his subjects possess one half of the commerce of Brasil, as the greater part of it is usurped by the English, to whom the best factories belong, under Portuguese names, and for whom the Portuguese traders, of which there are but few, act as brokers and agents. The troops which protect Brasil consist of about 7 or 8000 regular soldiers, and about 30 or 40,000 militia. Those of the mines of St. Paul pass for good troops; but this is a small army for so vast an extent of country, the northern part of which may be attacked with great advantage by the French. The colony of St. Sacrement is easily taken at the beginning of every war between the Spaniards and the Portuguese; and the method to prevent this, as well as to annoy the Spaniards, would be to yield this colony to the English. Though by thus giving themselves masters, the remedy would be worse than the disease.

If Brasil was vigorously attacked at the same

* From the coasts of Loango, Congo, Angola, and Benguela, but chiefly from the port of St. Philip de Benguela. T.

time, by the French, on the side of Para, of Maranham, and along the Rio Negro; and by the Spaniards on the side of Rio St. Pedro, advancing also towards St. Paul and the capitania of St. Vincent, its defence would be very difficult, as it would be assailed on the side of its mines. Any marine aid from the English would be of little use, and it would be equally dangerous for the Portuguese to suffer any English troops to land; a measure which they would never adopt but at the last extremity. The Portuguese, however, have no cause for alarm, while the French and Spanish colonies, which are contiguous to Brasil, are not better provided with troops, and the means of making hostile incursions.

CHAPTER V.

ISLANDS BELONGING TO PORTUGAL.

These islands may be divided into four parts. 1st. Porto Santo, and the island of Madeira. 2d. The Açores, or Terceiras. 3d. The Cape Verde islands. And 4th. Islands on the coast of Guinea.*

I.. PORTO SANTO AND MADEIRA.

The island of Porto Santo is situate 32° north latitude, eight nautic leagues to the north-east of the easternmost point of Madeira: it is not two leagues in length, and about half a league

---

* General Dumouriez has forgot in his enumeration the small but important island of Fernaô de Noronha, situated about sixty-four leagues to the north-east of Cape St. Roque in Brasil. In this island, inhabited by exiles, and where no women are suffered, the Portuguese keep a strong garrison; all the little sandy bays, as well as the anchoring places, being defended by forts, or intrenched batteries: it is about ten miles long, and between two or two and an half miles in breadth, has lenty of water, and produces an abundance of provisions. T.

in breadth: it lies about 160 leagues from Lisbon. This island was discovered by John Gonçalez Zarco, and Tristan Vaz. It contains 1200 inhabitants, the greater part of which reside in the town which bears its name. The bay is rather commodious, though exposed to the south and south-west winds.

The island of Madeira is 160 leagues from Lisbon, and about the same distance from the Açores. It lies in 32° 37′ to 53° north latitude, and is about thirteen leagues in length, and four leagues in its greatest breadth. It was discovered the same year as Porto Santo, and by the same John Gonçalez Zarco, who gave it the name of Madeira, from the quantity of wood which covered it. He set it on fire, and the conflagration lasted seven years. It is divided into two capitanias: that of Machico belongs to the house of Vimioso, and contains the little town of Machico, with 2000 inhabitants, the burgh of Santa Cruz with 1200, and seven villages which contain about 2 or 3000. The capitania of Funchal was given by King John I. to the house of Zarco, which is now become that of Camara, to which it belongs at this day. The capital of this district is Funchal. It is defended towards the sea by five forts on the main land, and a small fort on an island (the Loo castle), and towards the land by the castle of St. Joao do Pico (commonly Peak castle); it is an episcopal see. This island contains one city, four towns, and upwards of 120,000[*] inhabitants, divided into forty-three parishes. It is the constant residence of a governor; and the custom-house, with the tenths that the king derives from this island, as grand-master of the order of Christ, produces a revenue of upwards 300,000 crusades. The principal trade of this place is in honey, wax, dragon's-blood, sugar, excellent wine, and various kinds of fruit.[†]

2. THE AÇORES (AZORES) OR TERCEIRAS.

The Açores derive their name from a kind of bird that resembles a hawk, of which a prodigious quantity was found there, on their first discovery by the commander Alvarez de Cabral, in 1432. They were also called Terceiras, from the name of the principal island, which

---

[*] In the year 1768, the inhabitants living in these forty-three parishes amounted to 63,913, of whom there were 31,341 males, and 32,572 females. *Forster's Voyage round the World*, Vol. I. p. 16. T.

[†] The only survey ever engraved of Madeira and Porto Santo islands has been published by W. Faden, in 1791. T.

was the third in the line of discovery. The Flemings, who discovered them almost at the same time with the Portuguese, call them the Flemish Islands. They are nine in number. The first is Santa Maria: it is three leagues and a half in length, and three in breadth; has an harbour well fortified, with about 5000 inhabitants. The second is the island of St. Michael. It is fifteen leagues in length, from two to five in breadth, and is the most populous of these islands, as it contains upwards of 40,000 souls. It is extremely fertile, although the fiftieth part of it is not cultivated. It contains one city, five burghs, and twenty-two villages. The city is called Ponte Delgada. The house of Ribera Grande, to whom this island belongs, draws from it an income of more than 40,000* crusades. The third is the island Terceira, which is nine leagues long, and four in breadth: it contains one city, two burghs, and fifteen villages. Angra, the capital of it, is situated on the south coast of the island, and is a bishopric. The entrance into the harbour lies between two points which project into the sea. On the west point is a large rock, on which is

* About £2000.

seated the castle of St. John the Baptist, with an advanced bastion, called St. Antonio. This rock, which is of black stone, is called Le Mono, or the Ape. On the east point is the castle of St. Sebastian. The port has good anchorage, and is very secure against every wind but the south-east, which obliges the vessels to weigh anchor as soon as it begins to blow. The town is well situated, well built, with large streets, well paved, and decorated with fountains, and contains upwards of 10,000 inhabitants. It was erected into a city and a bishop's see in 1534, by John III. Its ordinary garrison consists of 500 men. It is very capable of defence, and well provided with artillery; it is said to have upwards of 180 brass cannon, and many of them forty-eight pounders: it also possesses the famous culverin of Malacca, which is a sixty pounder. The town of St. Sebastian has about 1000 inhabitants, and is defended by six well-conditioned forts. Here the senate of the island assembles when any affairs of importance require its deliberations. Villa Praya, or Praya, is two leagues to the north-east of Angra, situated on a safe and well-defended bay: it contains near 3000 souls. The fourth island is that of St. George, about three leagues to the westward of Terceira, being about nine leagues in length, and one and an half broad. It is high but flat, and at its two points there are two detached islots. Its port is safe for small vessels. It contains about 3000 souls, distributed in three burghs, and four villages, all of which are on the southern side of the island; the northern part being rocky and incapable of cultivation. The fifth is Graciosa, which lies four leagues to the north of St. George, and about seven north by west from Terceira; it is two leagues and an half long, and as many in breadth; the northern part has a better soil than that which is towards the south. It contains two burghs, and 3600 inhabitants. The sixth is the island of Fayal, which lies seventeen leagues to the west of Terceira. It forms a kind of lozenge, whose diagonals are each seven or eight leagues in length. The principal town is called Santa Cruz, and its road or harbour, Horta de Fayal. It contains 4000 inhabitants, divided into eleven parishes. The seventh, the island of Pico; is separated from Fayal by a channel, two leagues broad; is seven leagues in length, and four and an half in breadth. It is seen at the distance of fifteen leagues at sea, on account of a very high mountain, which is said to possess an elevation of three miles.* Its principal port is Villa das Lagens. Several others are dispersed round the coast, the principal of which is called Madalena, opposite to Fayal. This island is very fertile, and abounds in cedar trees. It contains two towns, four villages, and 2000 inhabitants. The eighth is the island of Florès, which is twelve miles long, and three broad. The principal place is Ribeira da Cruz, which contains 800 souls. It has altogether two burghs, four villages, and 2000 inhabitants. It gives the title of Marquis to the house of Gouvea. The ninth is the island of Corvo; is situate to the north of Florès, from which it is separated by a channel of nine miles in breadth. It is about eight or nine miles in circumference, has one parish, and about 500 inhabitants. The Açores contain about 80,000 souls, but have very little trade; so that the revenue which the King of Portugal derives from these islands is not equivalent to the expence of maintaining of them.

* This mountain, which is a volcano, is not supposed to be so high as the Peak of Teneriffe, whose elevation does not exceed two miles, or two miles and a quarter above the level of the sea. T.

3. CAPE VERD ISLANDS.

The Cape Verd Islands are situate at the distance of 110 leagues from the Cape of the same name, on the western coast of Africa, between 23 and 26° west long. and 15 and 18° north lat. They are supposed by some to be the ancient Hesperides of Pliny and Ptolemy. They were discovered, in the year 1460, by Antonio de Noli, a Genoese, under the direction of the Infant Don Henry, who presented them to King Alphonso V. his nephew. They are ten in number: the principal of them is St. Jago, about 12 leagues in length and 32 in circumference. Ribeira Grande, or St. Jago, which is a bishopric, has a port capable of receiving large vessels, with fourteen fathoms water at its entrance; but that of La Praya, called Porto Praya, and situated on the south side, like the former, is still better. This island has been twice attacked and pillaged; in 1582, during the war carried on for the succession of Don Sebastian, and in 1712, by a French squadron. The other islands are Mayo, Boavista, Sal, Fogo, Bravo, St. Nicholas, St. Lucia, St. Vincent, and St. Antonio. They are poor, subject to famine, and have but little trade, which consists chiefly in rice and salt;

nor does their combined population amount to more than 16,000 souls.

4. ISLANDS ON THE COAST OF GUINEA.

The person who discovered these islands is not known, though the period of their discovery is supposed to be about 1471, during the reign of Alphonso V. The principal of them is St. Thomas, which has a city, that is the residence of a bishop, and contains about 3000 inhabitants. The second is Prince's Island, and contains about 2000 inhabitants. The third is Fernaõ do Po,* so named from its discoverer, and which has very few people on it: and the fourth is Annobom, or Good Year, with not more than 300 inhabitants. These four islands are not only very poor, but equally unwholesome; and the anchorage not always safe. Their vicinity to the line prevents them from keeping any stock of fresh provisions; so that the ships which sometimes call there, instead of obtaining refreshments, are obliged themselves to relieve the inhabitants of these unfortunate islands.

* This island belongs now to the Spaniards, to whom it is as useless as it was to the Portuguese. T.

CHAPTER VI.

CONCLUSION.

THIS brief description of the Portuguese colonies is sufficient to give an adequate idea of their strength. The Asiatic colonies could not subsist, without bringing destruction on Portugal; though they had never been attacked by European enemies. The Mahometans dispersed along the shores of the Red Sea, and in the kingdom of Mogul, almost to the peninsula of Malacca, were too powerful not to destroy, in the end, the weak and ill-fortified establishments of the Portuguese. Too indolent and too proud to submit to the engagements of commerce, they were alone qualified to carry on war; and therefore could not repair, by the advantages of trade, the losses they sustained by the failure of their military operations. Their continual piracies excited a general indignation against them; while the Indian nations, in their own defence, were obliged to engage in the same practice of maritime depredation. Fanaticism excited them both. Jesus Christ and Mahomet were always invoked to give victory to their respective worshippers, in these unjust and bloody combats; in which their respective interests were blended with the glory of their respective religions. In the mean time the Indians learned the science of navigation and the art of war, and in a short time would have known as much as their masters. The French, the English, and the Dutch reaped the fruits of the Portuguese discoveries. They combined industry with strength, and have established those rich commercial companies, which are so powerful as to keep the Indians in awe, and to sustain extensive wars. The general outcry of the Indians against the Portuguese has justified the fury with which these different people have pillaged them without resistance. It was, however, the reign of the three Philips, and the bad administration of the Spaniards, which prevented the Portuguese from defending themselves. They were sacrificed by the court of Madrid, who regarded Portugal as a conquered country, and not entitled to the privileges of the rest of its dominions.

Brasil has been retarded in its population and its cultivation by the spirit of chivalry, which considered it as a degradation to become a cultivator of land and a colonist. Riches were acquired with more rapidity and éclat in the East Indies: piracy opened a career more attractive to a brave, proud, and indolent people. The kings of Portugal indulged the prejudices of their subjects in appearing to despise Brasil, which was therefore peopled only with villains and vagabonds; and finding that it produced no addition to their revenues, they granted whole provinces to individuals, who subjected the labour and exertions of the inhabitants to their own advantage, and strangled in its birth the spirit of industry and enterprize. The Dutch, in 1624, found Brasil in a poor and uncultivated state, when they established at Fernambucco a colony, upon the same principles as those they had formed in the East Indies. Here they gave to the Portuguese an example of industry; and though, after a war of thirty years, when they were obliged to abandon this colony, they destroyed their plantations and factories. The Portuguese availed themselves, in some degree, of their example, and being supported by the English, advanced Brasil to the condition in which it is at this day. Indeed, since the loss of their Oriental possessions, their commercial speculations have been directed to this quarter. The government has withdrawn from the hands of individuals a great part of the provinces: but this measure has been carried too far, and avidity is always blind. The establishment of companies has also given a severe blow to the prosperity of Brasil. The inhabitants, who live in a state of oppression, are disposed to revolt. Burdensome taxes check the spirit of industry, and spread around discouragement and despair. Among other well-combined means to recall public confidence and industry, it is necessary to employ mildness with discretion. Power may enforce submission, but it cannot command industry. If troops are to be employed in keeping distant possessions in subjection, it is equally dangerous to send too many or too few. The example of the English colonies in resisting the stamp act, has produced a powerful effect upon the European colonies of America. It is the cause of all the disorders which exist in Mexico, Peru, and Brasil.

The island of Madeira is the most populous and opulent of the Portuguese settlements; but it is not the most productive to the mother country. The inhabitants stand in little need of supplies from Europe, carry on a direct trade with England, and pay but trifling duties to the king. The other islands and colonies in Africa are in a very wretched condition. The number and extent of the Portuguese colonies may be imposing; but their real condition will appear from the following state of their population.—

	Inhabitants.
In Asia	50,000
Africa	80,000
Brasil	430,000
Madeira and Porto Santo	*130,000
The Açores	80,000
Cape Verd Islands	16,000
Islands on the coast of Guinea	5,000
	791,000

Of these the Portuguese scarce form a sixth part. The small proportion of this population

* See the note at the bottom of p. 90.

to the immense extent of the Portuguese settlements is a sufficient indication of their weakness, and justifies the conclusion, that the commerce and marine of Portugal are in a very
bad condition.

BOOK III.

THE ARMY.

CHAPTER I.

DEFECTS OF THE PORTUGUESE ARMY.

THE Portuguese army has been in a most contemptible state for a century to the period of the war of 1762. In consequence of fifty years of peace, a most destructive earthquake, several famines, and a most abominable conspiracy, it had been totally neglected, and was sunk into the most wretched condition. It was composed of from 8 to 10,000 men, of a class inferior to peasants; without uniforms, without arms, begging alms or assassinating for a livelihood; and the officers of these troops were servants, who mounted behind the carriages, or served at the tables of their masters, when they were not on duty. This is the unexaggerated and inconceivable picture of the Portuguese troops, before the war of 1762, and the arrival of Count de Lippe, who instantly set about reforming the whole of it.

The Portuguese are naturally indisposed to application. The Great are averse to military employments; and as, in consequence of its frequent revolutions, this government is full of suspicion, it is permitted but to certain families to enter into the army. Strangers alone can support its character, and they are generally ill chosen, and treated with indignity. The obligations which the Portuguese have received from foreigners, since the year 1640, cannot be equalled but by their ingratitude. It seems to be a principle with these people, to demand their assistance in time of war, to redeem the follies they have committed during a period of peace. A military zeal and ardour seems to return on the arrival of these auxiliaries: but when the war is closed, their zeal is extinguished, their arms are suffered to rust, and these foreigners, to whom they owed so much, die or desert, oppressed by injustice, by debts, and despair; while the Portuguese sink into their former state of ignorance and torpor. This absurd conduct has been frequently renewed since the epocha that has been just mentioned, and it is probable that it will be again repeated. Unfortunately for the state which is governed by a single minister, that minister is never qualified for every department, and therefore gives his attention to those in which his capacity has been chiefly exercised. The Count d'Oeyras, first minister of Portugal, is a mere politician, and is altogether uninformed in military matters. Besides, he is an enemy to the character of a soldier, which requires resolution and vigour; qualities by no means requisite, in his opinion, to improve that obedience and submission which are essential to his government.

The army of Portugal has a very respectable appearance; but the officers are ill chosen, ill paid, and nevertheless are entirely engaged by interest, with the least spark of military honour. Their exterior appearance, however, is under some kind of regulation, and the cut of their clothes, as well as their manual exercise, is in the Prussian method.

The Count de Lippe has rendered an essential service to Portugal, in new modelling its army; but he remained there too short a time to carry his reform into effect; besides, he did not make a proper choice of officers to finish the work which he had begun.

When war was declared in 1762, Portugal finding itself without officers, and without soldiers, the government, alarmed at its defenceless situation, employed every means to engage foreign officers in its service. A crowd of military adventurers, therefore, who had been dishonoured in, or driven from, the service of other powers, were received in the Portuguese army. Mr. Mello, ambassador from the court of Lisbon to that of London, was commissioned to receive all who offered; and rank as well as money was held forth to tempt military men, of any character or country, to engage with the court of Lisbon. Instead of applying to the King of Prussia, or the Dutch, for a body of able and tried officers; instead of holding forth adequate remunerations to military men of merit of any nation, the Portuguese government introduced into its army a great number of foreigners, whose vices and ignorance tended to increase the disorder and pusillanimous spirit which prevailed in it. This evil was cured by a very violent remedy. The minister, having dissembled his resentment at these abuses during the war, which were so evident, that they even forced themselves upon his observation, employed an expedient as fatal as the abuses themselves, by persecuting and driving out of the kingdom every foreign officer without distinction. As to the Portuguese officers, their pay does not enable them to live better than the common soldiers, whose comrades and relations they are. The subaltern posts are filled from among the inferior classes; and their hatred of foreigners, arising from their having one-half more pay than themselves, prevents their associating with, or receiving any improvement from them; and hence it is that they remain in ignorance and wretchedness.

The Portuguese soldier is obedient, patient, robust, lively, and dexterous; but he is, at the same time, idle, filthy, and disposed to find fault with every thing: but he is capable, when properly attended to, of doing credit to his character. His aversion to the Spaniards should be encouraged, but he should be made to comprehend, that he cannot gain any advantage over the superior numbers of that nation, but by superior discipline. The mutual contempt which these nations entertain for each other, arises from their ignorance and their presumption. It is very extraordinary, when it is their mutual interest to know each other, that their reciprocal aversion should operate so powerfully as to prevent any useful communication between them. Hence it is that a war between Spain and Portugal, will consist of little more than groping about in the dark, because neither the one nor the other have maps, or guides, or spies.

These defects of the military establishments in Portugal might have been easily corrected by the Count de Lippe. But to attain such an object, a full power and the exercise of a rigid discipline was indispensable. It would be also necessary to make the appointments of the Portuguese officers equal to those of the foreign officers, in order to dissipate the grovelling jealousies and contempt that subsist between them, and to make talents the only distinction; at the same time to encourage the foreign officers, who live in a continual state of suspicion and distrust, by making them equal sharers in the favour of government, and attaching them to the country by solid establishments. In short, it would be the best policy to reward diligence by attaching to it honour as well as emolument, and to punish indolence by disgrace and the loss of fortune.

CHAPTER II.

STATE OF THE ARMY.—INFANTRY, CAVALRY, LIGHT TROOPS, ARTILLERY, AND FORTIFICATIONS.

The state of the Portuguese army, independent of its marine and its colonies, consists of 33 battalions, containing 26,000 infantry, and 26 squadrons, which compose about 4000 cavalry. The peasantry also form a militia of upwards of 100,000 men, who serve without pay, but engage with great fury, and are very formidable to the Spaniards, by their manner of fighting; as, from the ignorance of their generals, the neglect of their officers, and the want of discipline in the soldiers, the latter are ever exposed to ambuscades, assassinations, and sudden attacks.

The Portuguese army is in a tolerable state of discipline: it marches and manœuvres well; but it ought more frequently to be drawn out into encampments, that the little manœuvres of exercise might be applied to the great operations of war. The battalions are composed of seven companies, one of which consists of grenadiers, of 140 men each. This formation is imperfect, according to the rules of tactics, as it is not capable of square divisions, without confusion. There are many other faults in its evolutions, the greater part of which proceed from the same principle. Neither are the troops accustomed to remove earth, to practise the manœuvres of attack and defence, as well as the art of fortification; and all this is essential in a country like Portugal, where war must be on the defensive, and carried on in detail. The infantry of the north is very superior in discipline, as well as in stature, to that of the south, especially of the capital and of Elvas.

The cavalry is well mounted on horses from Andalusia, Beira, and Traz os Montes; which are of a moderate height, like those of the Spanish cavalry; but they are all geldings.

It is a problem which experience alone can resolve, whether the gelding or the stone-horse is best qualified for the service of cavalry; and if the quiet disposition of the one is equal, in point of effect, to the ardent spirit of the other. The Spanish cavalry is the only one in Europe which consists of stone-horses, and it is of acknowledged excellence; but it may be doubted whether it possesses sufficient solidity to support a line of infantry. Cavalry should possess these four qualities; order, solidity, force, and swiftness. The Spanish cavalry are famous for the two latter, and the Portuguese possess the two former. The union of these four qualities are by no means incompatible; but I have my doubts whether they are to be found in any cavalry of any nation.

Portugal maintains twelve squadrons of cuirassiers in pretty good condition and discipline. Though I am rather doubtful whether they possess sufficient solidity to resist the impetuous shock of the Spanish cavalry, from the moderate size of their horses. Their breastplates, however, give them two incontestable advantages; though the Spaniards are of a different opinion, as they never make use of them. The first is, that they afford protection to the soldier; and secondly, they give him an idea of his superiority over troops who are not clad in such defensive armour. The Portuguese dragoons, however, will never equal those of Spain.

It is a great advantage to this cavalry to keep always in close union with the infantry, and never to engage alone in the plains of

Alemtejo, and still less in those of Estremadura, because there is great reason to conjecture that it would fail in an engagement with Spanish cavalry. Its most advantageous place is in the line, where it would be able to support the infantry; and in battle it is better calculated to maintain its ranks, to cover a retreat, or protect the forage. It would execute with less activity, but with more certainty, the great manœuvres as well as the detail of its service. The squadron has the same defect as in Spain, in being composed of four companies, which require too many officers, and renders the establishment expensive. A company of cavalry is worth in the provinces near £500. per annum. The regiments which are on court duty are very much harassed, because they do the duty of body guards, and that the king, whom they constantly attend, always goes full speed; so that they must be necessarily in worse condition, and the companies of less value.

The Portuguese cavalry has this advantage over that of Spain, that it is exercised in firing, and accustomed to leap hedges and ditches in squadrons; a manœuvre which the Spaniards can scarcely believe; but which they could execute better than any other cavalry, if they were exercised in it.

There is but one regiment of light dragoons, of about 1200 men, very ill exercised, and of course incapable of engaging in that kind of war for which they are designed. The colonel, though a good officer, is not sufficiently active to conduct light troops. Colonel Louis Hollard is the only officer capable of that service in Portugal. It is, nevertheless, indispensable to have a body of from 5 to 6000 light troops in a war with Spain, which being defensive, the only attacks that the Portuguese can make must be by way of incursion.

The artillery is composed of three battalions, but in a very bad state of discipline. The cannon are ill made and clumsy. The minister had the good fortune to engage two excellent founders, brought up under the famous Maritz; but the prevailing prejudice against foreigners has got the better of actual want, and, in consequence of ill treatment, they have been obliged to desert from the service. There are no field pieces, nor any small cannon, to accompany the infantry; which would be of the greatest use in such a country as Portugal, where there is a post at every step. There are three colonels of artillery; Colonel York, an Englishman, who contributed so much to the taking of the Havannah; Colonel Macbean, a Scotchman, who distinguished himself in the allied army in Westphalia; and Lieutenant Colonel Hollard, a Swiss, but who has been both in the service of Prussia and Denmark, and is well known by his valour and services. He is the only person capable of putting the artillery of Portugal upon a good footing; though he would be employed more essentially in forming a body of light troops.

The corps of engineers is ill formed, and extremely ignorant; they can do little more than rule paper and page a register. Nevertheless there are two engineers of great reputation among them; Funck, a Swede, who served with distinction under Marshal Saxe, and Miron, a Swiss, a brave and most excellent officer; who was menaced with a trial, for having attempted to restore the fortifications of Almeida, and to defend it against the Spaniards, in 1762. But the cowardice of the governor served as his justification. The School of Engineers is in a very backward state, and in 1766, its most forward scholars had not got beyond the second book of Euclid.

The Portuguese might avail themselves of their foreign engineers to procure correct maps of their country, in which they are totally deficient; at least they might obtain topographical surveys of the chains of mountains, of rivers, vallies, and frontier plains, that every post might be known in case of war. It is said that the Count de Lippe made himself well acquainted with the country which he passed through in 1762, and that he was actually engaged in making maps of it. General Fraser has, since that time, made a tour through the northern division of the kingdom; but he had only draftsmen with him, and I much doubt whether he viewed it with the eye of a master. Colonel Funck has also been employed to make designs of the frontiers; and he presented to the minister a plan of general fortification, which is supposed to have been accepted.

CHAPTER III.

GENERALS, THE STAFF, OFFICERS, &c. SUBSISTENCE, THE MINISTER OF WAR.

The Count de Lippe is the restorer of the military art in this country. He is equally amiable, witty, learned, brave, and virtuous. He is intimately acquainted with the sublime parts of war, well skilled in tactics, and a good engineer. He will acquire an high degree of reputation, at the head of the Portuguese troops, if he will cease to neglect them, and return again to re-establish those parts of the army which have fallen into disorder since his absence, and to complete the work which he began, with an equal degree of zeal and success.

The second general is an old Portuguese devotee, the Count Baron of Arcos: he lets every thing go to destruction, because he is incapable of applying a remedy to any thing.

The first lieutenant-general is a Scotch gentleman, Simon Fraser, the son of Lord Lovat.

He is young, and served only two years in Canada, as colonel of a regiment of Scotch Highlanders, after having been a barrister at law during the former part of his life. He has a great share of ambition, undaunted courage, a great deal of presumption, and very moderate talents.

There are two field-marshals of distinguished character: a German, named Bohm, a creature of the Count de Lippe, a brave and well informed officer, but rather too much of a courtier; and a Scotchman, named Macklean, a brave and ancient officer, and an excellent commander of infantry. The rest of the staff are Portuguese, with little or no military qualifications, and whose names are scarcely known. The court of Lisbon, therefore, ought to procure better, and fix them in its service by just and honourable treatment.

There are some colonels, lieutenant-colonels, and majors, who are good officers, but they almost all of them strangers. Colonel Smith, an Englishman, passes for a good engineer, as well as commander of cavalry; Macdonnell, Fitzgerald, Campbell, Forbes, and Chauncey, are good officers. There are also some Portuguese noblemen, of whom there are great hopes, from their zeal and their talents: they are the Marquis de Lavradio, the Counts de Prado, and d'Aponte, Deluis de Miranda, Pinto, Acunha, &c.

There is no staff in the Portuguese army, nor in that of Spain. The post of major-general of the army was last held by a Scotchman, named Preston, who retired from the service at the time of the unfortunate affair of Colonel Graveron. This post has been supplied by two inspectors of the troops. The employment of quarter-master-general is very difficult to fulfil: it is his business to issue all the orders; to provide for every undertaking, whether it relates to military operations, or to subsistence; to arrange, direct, and conduct the passage and movements of the troops, to form maps, and to keep all the archives of the war. There is neither in Spain nor in Portugal, companies of guides, nor a train of waggons laden with pontoons, planks, &c. There is no military board, or any fixed regulations for provisions or forage. The great number of places, and the small extent of the theatre of war in Portugal, render this defect less likely to be felt; at the same time the troops always run some risk of dying with hunger.

A commissary named Ferrari, lately passed

from the service of Spain into that of Portugal, who regulated the making of bread for the troops, so as to gain 33 per cent. for the government; and in case of a future war, he will, probably, be appointed commissary-general of the army.

The scarcity of forage will always prevent the Portuguese from keeping the field, and maintaining a large body of cavalry; and this circumstance proceeds from a defective state of agriculture. Nevertheless, the supplies for a Portuguese army might be easily collected in two or three strong places in the back parts, from whence they might be drawn with convenience and safety.

The military hospitals form no concern of the king, as a community of monks always charge themselves with that branch of military administration. But regular and fixed hospitals would be more serviceable, and might be contrived.

One of the principal obstacles to the due regulation of subsistence during war, is the manner of conducting it, at least, to the present time. As soon as the Spaniards enter Portugal, the king publishes a declaration, by which he enjoins his subjects to fall upon the invaders, and the national hatred excites them to execute this ordinance. The Spanish army always pushes on; the villages are depopulated, and their inhabitants fall back upon the capital. The peasants arrive there in crowds, with their wives and children; so that the king, who should have nothing more than his army to maintain, finds, at the end of two or three months of the campaign, two or three hundred thousand additional mouths to feed. Another resulting evil is, that the court of Madrid avails itself of the famine which is occasioned by its invading army, induces the Portuguese peasants by kind treatment to abandon their own country, or transport them by force into different provinces of Spain, with their wives, children, and cattle.

To remedy this evil, it would be necessary to regulate the number of militia in time of war, and to prohibit any peasants to resist the enemy, to abandon their villages, or to disobey the conqueror, to whom they, of course, belong, till the force of arms, or returning peace, delivers them from a foreign yoke. But whatever the Spaniards may say to the contrary, this war of the peasantry is by no means important, but to ignorant and undisciplined troops. The burning of two or three villages, and the hanging of as many monks or curates, or principal persons in the parish, quickly puts a stop to the indiscreet and barbarous fury of the country people.

A king of Portugal, who has found the means of regulating his expences by his revenue, will be able to sustain a war, upon equal if not superior terms against Spain. The article of subsistence is the principal and most expensive; every attention therefore should be given to this fundamental object. Established magazines, and economy in the dispensation of them, form the basis and strength of that defence which is required for this little kingdom.

The war department is not under proper regulations, and its official proceedings are dilatory. The advanced age of the Count d'Oeyras is a public inconvenience. He is continually occupied in various less important objects, to which he sacrifices his precious time. The minister of war is Don Louis d'Acunha; a man of honour, but of little credit, and who does nothing. He is scarcely known by one half of the military officers. All the real business is in the hands of a confidential person, and secretary of Count d'Oeyras, Don Miguel d'Arriaga, he is a man of great merit, integrity, and understanding; but he is only the echo of the count, and that minister being of a dilatory character, no advantage is derived from his superintendance, so that the administration of the army is every year becoming worse and worse. It is divided into two departments; that of the north, which comprehends the three provinces of Entre Minho e Douro, Traz os Montes, and Beira; and that of the south, which embraces Estremadura, Alemtejo, and Algarve.

CHAPTER IV.

TOPOGRAPHY, RIVERS, MOUNTAINS, FORTIFIED PLACES.

Topography, or a knowledge of the position of places; of the course and current of rivers; of the extent and inclination of chains of mountains; and the situation of fortified places, is the first branch of military science, and a necessary part of the detail of a kingdom in a state of war. An enemy must be acquainted with these natural or artificial barriers, either to avoid or surmount them; while the citizen ought to know them still better, to employ them as the means of defence. But this grand and leading branch of the science of war, is not duly considered by many nations, particularly those of Spain and Portugal, who have not carried on one single scientific campaign against each other, since the foundation of their respective kingdoms.

Portugal is watered by four principal rivers, which may serve to direct both its offensive and defensive operations. One of these rivers, the Guadiana, which runs from the east to the south-west and south; enters into Portugal between Xerumena and Olivença, in Alemtejo, and serves, in its course, as a natural ditch to that province and the little kingdom of Algarve, dividing the latter from Andalusia. Though the Guadiana is a considerable river, it cannot be employed to any purposes of utility in the present war, from the small importance of the provinces through which it flows, and because it is incapable of being navigated by boats for more than thirty-six miles, from Mertola to the sea. The other rivers run from east to west. The Minho divides a part of Galicia from a part of Entre Minho e Douro; but it does not serve as the least defence to the latter province, which may be attacked without crossing this river. The Douro, coming from the kingdom of Leon, enters Portugal; and, after dividing it, empties itself into the sea, near the city of Oporto. It is navigable by boats from Lamego, a course of above fifty miles; its banks are rich, and it may be rendered very serviceable if that place should be the object of military operations. But the most important river of Portugal, the key of Lisbon, and the nursing mother of those armies which enter into that kingdom, is the Tagus. For about seventy-two miles from Alcantara to Abrantes, its course is interrupted by rocks and falls, and consequently incapable of navigation: but from Abrantes to the sea, which is ninety miles; it is navigable by vessels of considerable burden, which may convey all the necessary supplies of war. Its right bank, though mountainous, is very abundant in provisions and cattle, and is covered with villages; while the left is marshy and barren. From Santarem, upon the right bank, to Lisbon, a distance of fifty miles, the declivity is so great, that the first of these towns commands the latter, and is the key of the country. Several small rivers discharge themselves into the Tagus; the principal of which are the Elga, (which divides Beira from Spain) the Ponsul, the Laca, the Zezere, and the Rio Mayor. This state of the country increases the means of defence, and the difficulties of attack. All these small rivers, which descend from the mountains of Beira are very unequal and dangerous in their course; sometimes they appear only as shallow brooks, and sometimes as rapid torrents, which inundate the adjoining country. The Count de Lippe, in 1762, being encamped at Punhete, after the march of the Spaniards towards Villa Velha, and having the Zezere, with its bridges, in his rear; this river, in consequence of violent rains, was so greatly increased, that the bridges were broken down, and he found himself inclosed, without resource, between the Tagus and the Zezere. If the Spaniards had known, or could have imagined this event, (and a knowledge of the country would have informed them of it,) they would have taken him and his whole army without the discharge of a single musket.

The Spaniards discovered little or no knowledge of the position of the mountains of Portugal, their chains, their extent, their heights, or their defiles: when they attempted to penetrate to Oporto by the Traz os Montes; they were ignorant that the two chains of mountains of Marom and of Geres, form an insurmountable barrier between this province and that of Oporto: and that to pass from Chaves to Oporto, it is absolutely necessary to procure the native guides, with their mules, which, accustomed to this journey, pass through narrow ways covered with wood, and on the brink of horrid precipices, where fifty peasants might stop the march of an army. In the same manner, when, after the taking of Almeida, the Spaniards had advanced to Guarda, to get in a straight line to Lisbon by Coimbra; they were ignorant that the Serra or mountain of Estrella, formed an impenetrable barrier, and that they must either return to the banks of the Tagus, or by keeping along the Douro, regain the sea shore, and thus form a march of two sides of a triangle to get round the Serra da Estrella.

Portugal is very mountainous. The province of Alemtejo alone is varied by plains, which has been considered as an inducement to make it the theatre of war, forgetful of the true system, that is, to suit the war to the country, and not the country to the war.

All the mountains of the Spanish peninsula, are ramifications of the Pyrenees, which, taking different directions, on one side extend to the ocean, which they enter by Galicia and Portugal; and on the other to the Mediterranean sea, which they cross to Africa, forming by their summits the various islands that appear between Spain and the African continent.

The particular branches of these mountains, which pass into Portugal, run from east to west. The mountains which enter it by a part of Galicia and Leon, rather incline to the south; and they all form a natural barrier to the Portuguese provinces. The mountain of Geres and that of Marom, divide the Entre Minho e Douro from Traz os Montes: their branches extend as far as Beira, where they are denominated Serra de Alcoba and Serra da Estrella. Other ramifications of the mountains of Guadarama, which separate the Old from the New Castile, traverse the kingdom of Leon, and stretching onwards, under the name of Sierra de Gata, enter Portugal by the districts of Sabugal, Pena Macor and Castel Branco, continuing their course also by Guarda, Viseu and Coimbra.

On the left bank of the Tagus, are branches of the Sierra Morena and the Sierra Constantina, which enter Alemtejo by the way of Moura and Serpa; and which form several ridges, terminating at the Guadiana, the principal of which is the Serra de Aroche. (On the other side of the Guadiana, the chain continues through the kingdom of Algarve, which it divides from Alemtejo, and runs as far as Cape St. Vincent, and parallel to the south coast of Portugal, under the names of Serra de Caldeirao and Serra de Monchique.)

Portugal is so far from being deficient in fortified places, that it possesses more than are necessary for its protection; for if they were all sufficiently garrisoned, its army would be so weakened as not to be able to maintain a campaign. The inspection of fortified places is divided into two departments.

The province of Beira has not so many strong places as Alemtejo; but it is nevertheless almost impenetrable. The town of Almeida, taken in 1762, possesses considerable strength, and it will be still stronger from the repair of its works now carrying on by Colonel Funck. But this town does not cover Lisbon, and serves only to guard the entrance into the upper Beira, which the Spanish army can have no inducement to obtain.

That part of the country, which comprehends Zebreira, (where the construction of a fort has been projected,) Idanha, Pena Macor, and Alfayates, is the most necessary to defend, which can be done with the least difficulty, from its own natural strength. Nature has formed it to be a front to a Portuguese army, and has marked out the places to be guarded. It would be very difficult to penetrate into it, an entrance can only be obtained through defiles, which are almost impracticable, though they were not defended.

The province of Traz os Montes has no

strong places that are capable of defence. But the Spaniards well know, by fatal experience, the consequence of carrying their arms into a province, at once barren, mountainous, and difficult of access. Its strong places have been constructed in low situations, which are commanded on all sides, such as Miranda, Outeiro, Bragança and Chaves. This province is intersected by rivers, hollow ways, and mountains; particularly that of Marom, which covers Oporto, Braga, and the province of Entre Minho e Douro.

Entre Minho e Douro, possesses two principal places, Valença and Monçao, which are but ill fortified, but whose condition will be immediately improved on a new plan. It is full of small forts and ancient castles, the remains of former wars, which may serve as posts to check an attempt of the enemy to penetrate to Oporto. That city is entirely open and very opulent, and while it is the only object of an invasion on that side, is well worth an attempt. At the mouth of the Minho is the small town of Caminha, a regular fortification, but commanded on all sides. A chef d'œuvre of scientific infatuation.

The strongest and most important place in

the southern division, or the left side of the Tagus, and indeed of all Portugal, is Elvas; because the Spaniards cannot penetrate into Alemtejo and leave this place behind them: as well as Almeida, it requires so numerous a garrison, as to prove an inconvenient diminution of the strength of the army. It is an ancient place, with irregular bastions, and a cordon commanded by two mountains, upon which have been constructed the forts La Lippe and St. Lucia. The town rises like an amphi-theatre between them. The fort of La Lippe is independent of the place: it is a square, with four bastions, and an horn-work that is continued to the back of the mountain, and strengthened by several exterior works. It is very strong, in a very elevated position, and provided with casemates which are bomb-proof: almost all its batteries are covered, and it would be nearly impossible to raze its works. Nevertheless, this fort has great defects; many of its batteries are in the rock, and would soon be dismantled by a powerful cannonade. The declivity of the mountain is strengthened by mines, but their branches are easily discovered by observing the veins of earth across the rock. This side, therefore, although the most fortified, is very susceptible of attack, as it possesses the common fault of all horn-works, which carry the defences to too great a distance: at the same time, this fort garrisoned with 2000 men, might sustain a long siege. It commands also, the country and the town. The fort St. Lucia is composed of very ancient indefensible works, and might be taken with the greatest ease. The Spaniards might establish themselves in it during the whole war, burn or take the town and block up the garrison of fort La Lippe, which would then become entirely useless.

There are many ancient places, and of little importance, between the Tagus and the Guadiana. The left bank of the latter river is covered with them. These places were of great use in former wars, and are not altogether useless in those of the present time; because the taking of them will, at all events, cost time and money, interrupt the progress of an enemy, and would be attended with no advantage.

The leading object of the Portuguese, in a war with Spain, should be to cover both sides of the Tagus; and for this purpose, Castello de Vide on the left bank presents an excellent position. This is well known; and Funck has offered a plan for fortifying it, which has been accepted.

The post of Olivença, on the side of Spain, without being very interesting, may be very offensive to the Spaniards, because it favours the incursion of light troops into their Estremadura and Andalusia, and affords them a safe retreat, in the same manner as Moura, Mourao and Serpa.

The sea coast is defended by Setuval and the fort Sagres, at the point of Cape St. Vincent. Algarve is impenetrable, and the islands of Tavira, behind which ships, in time of war, may be secure from privateers, are fortified, though they received considerable injury from the great earthquake. Estremoz, as well as Evora and Beja, have no defence but the old walls with which they are invested.

Portugal has about fifteen or twenty strong places, and not more than 8 or 10,000 men to garrison them, without disabling its army from keeping the field.

The army of Portugal is more respectable than the Spaniards imagine, because they judge from the condition in which they saw it during the last war.

CHAPTER V.

HISTORICAL REFLECTIONS ON THE WAR OF PORTUGAL.

It is with astonishment we read in the page of history that the Spaniards have almost always been beat by the Portuguese. On a near examination of the two people, it appears that a greater degree of contempt than hatred subsists between them. This contempt of the Spaniards does not, however, appear to be consistent with their fatal experience of Portuguese valour. It seems to be an innate infatuation in the Spaniards to afford such a certain advantage to the Portuguese, who must be subdued, without resource, by the arms of that courageous people, if they employed in their wars against Portugal the same understanding that they manifest against the other nations of Europe, whom they respect more. It appears also from history, that this contempt does not arise from any predominant principle, but is itself the fundamental cause of that continual disgrace which the Spaniards have suffered whenever they have carried their arms into Portugal.

The most famous event in the ancient wars between these two nations is, the battle of Aljibarotta, in 1385. Portugal, ill governed by King Ferdinand, had sustained an unfortunate war against the King of Castile, Henry of Transtamare. This brave prince had just gained, sword in hand, a crown which did not belong to him by right of blood, but to which he was called by the general wish of the Castilians, and the hatred of the nation against Peter the Cruel. Ferdinand, giddy, inconstant, without merit, and without courage, governed by his mistress Leonora Telles de Menezes, whom he had carried off from her husband, Don Pedro d'Acunha, in order to marry her, drew down upon Portugal the arms of that hero, on inconsiderately taking part with the Duke of Lancaster, who disputed with him the crown of Castile, in right of his wife Constance. The Portuguese fleets were beaten; Don Pedro Rui Sarmiento overcame the Portuguese on the frontiers of Galicia; Henry himself took Viseu; raised the siege of Coimbra, from a spirit of gallantry, because the Queen Leonora lay-in there, and burned Lisbon in 1374. At length

Ferdinand, incapable of defending his kingdom, and being apprehensive of losing it altogether, had recourse to the Pope, by whose intervention the necessary peace was concluded; by which he abandoned the alliance of England for that of France, who was the ally of Spain; and he receiyed from the generosity of his conqueror all the towns which had been taken from him. The inconstant Ferdinand, after having passed his life in making and breaking treaties, in exciting the vengeance of Castile against his kingdom, and opposing it only with cowardice and humiliation, died in 1383, leaving an only daughter, named Beatrice, married to John I. King of Castile. There remained but one legitimate prince, the son of the King Don Pedro the Just, and of the unfortunate Inès de Castro: but this prince was odious to the Portuguese for having stabbed his wife in an excess of jealousy; and besides, he was a prisoner in Castile. The wicked Queen Leonora, the mother of Beatrice, was declared regent of the kingdom; she only wished to govern in the name of her daughter, without King John or the Castilians coming into Portugal.

Such was the position of Portugal, when two extraordinary men arose, who changed the face of the kingdom, and restored its power and its glory. John, the illegitimate son of Don Pedro the Just, grandmaster of the order of Avis, assisted by Nunho Alvares Pereira, the hero of his age, immediately declared himself regent of the kingdom. He began, in order to obtain the favour of the people, by stabbing, in the arms of Queen Leonora, the Count Andeyro, her lover, who governed tyrannically in her name. The queen regent called to her succour John I. who caused her to be arrested, and conducted as a prisoner to Tordesillas; from thence he went to lay siege to Lisbon, in 1384. The grandmaster threw himself into that city, with an handful of brave men, and sustained the siege, with great courage, against a formidable army. The plague, brought on by disease and famine, prevailed in the Castilian army; but the king being obstinately bent on continuing the siege, lost, by this calamity, two grandmasters of the order of St. James, the grand commander, the admiral, the two marshals of Castile, Don Pedro de Lara, the flower of his knights, and upwards of 30,000 men. Being thus deprived of his army, he at length raised the siege, and was pursued in his retreat by the intrepid grandmaster. He did not succeed better in procuring the assassination of that hero; the conspiracy was discovered, and the conspirators punished with death. The Portuguese also gained a considerable victory at Trancoso, against the Archbishop of Toledo. At length, Pereira assembled the states of the kingdom at Coimbra, and prevailed on them to elect the grandmaster king, to the prejudice of Beatrice and Prince John. The King of Castile re-entered Portugal at the head of a fine army of 46,000 men. He took the route of the Tagus, as the shortest, advanced by Abrantes and Santarem, and arrived without the least opposition at Algibarrota, where his intrepid rival waited his coming. The Portuguese army consisted of no more than 10,000 men, but they were encouraged by the spirit of national hatred, by their late successes, and by their confidence in the two heroes who commanded them. The Castilians, trusting to their superior numbers, considered themselves as proceeding to certain victory, and the unresisting conquest of the small body of Portuguese which appeared against them. So blinded were they with these expectations, that they detached the greatest part of their cavalry to make a circuit by Alcanhede, in order to attack the enemy in the rear, and seize on all the fugitives who might try to escape towards the capital. The advice of John de Rie, the French ambassador, was rejected with indignation, who advised the Castilian monarch to avoid an engagement, and to content himself with surrounding the enemy's camp, and to cut off their supplies. But the young courtiers accused the old warriors, who supported these opinions, of cowardice; and at length King John, hurried on by popular outcry, gave battle, August 14, 1385. The Castilians overcome with heat and fatigue, after having fasted for twenty-four hours, and without allowing themselves the least repose, attacked, with equal impetuosity and disorder. The Portuguese, who, being advantageously posted, in full vigour, and ably commanded, broke in upon them on all sides. The defeat immediately followed the attack, and the battle, which lasted but half an hour, left 10,000 Castilians dead on the field; three princes of the blood, Don John, Ferdinand of Castile, and Don Pedro of Aragon, the ambassador of France, and the flower of the nobility lost their lives, in a vain endeavour to rally the Castilians, who, being seized with a sudden panic, had abandoned themselves to a disgraceful flight. The enraged Portuguese gave no quarter; and the rest of the Castilian army would have perished, but for the arrival of the Infant of Navarre, who came to join them with a body of his troops, and for whom they were too impatient to wait, ere they engaged the enemy. This prince collected the remains of the routed army, and led them back into Spain. The king fled, almost alone, upon a mule, on which he continued his flight for thirteen leagues without stopping; and did not think himself in safety till he arrived at Seville. The new sovereign of Portugal strengthened his throne by successive victories, and at length granted peace to the Castilians in 1389.

This war is the most unfortunate that the Spaniards have made in Portugal; nevertheless it is, perhaps, the only one in which they have conducted their operations with skill and judgment. The object was to get possession of the kingdom, and they accordingly considered the capital as the central point, and the grand object of attack: they therefore marched straight forward to it, without paying attention to any places which were out of their road thither, and followed the course of the Tagus as the shortest route. But fortune was not propitious to this plan of the war, and in its executive details some fatal errors were committed. During the siege of Lisbon, a dreadful pestilence attacked the Castilian army; and, in the second expedition, a spirit of precipitation, and an unreflecting confidence, incited King John to follow the counsels of his young courtiers, who were eager for battle; so that his army engaged with that disorder and temerity which led to a certain defeat. But without the accidental misfortune of the plague in 1384, Lisbon must have surrendered, and the kingdom have submitted to King John; who, on this occasion, can only be blamed for his obstinacy in continuing the siege, while sickness and famine weakened his army. As to the battle of Algibarrota, if, instead of engaging, King John had resolved to starve the camp of the Portuguese, and to wait for the succours of the Infant of Navarre, the grandmaster of Avis must have submitted at discretion, and the war would have been terminated without any effusion of blood. These were fatal errors; nevertheless the plan of the campaign was formed with knowledge and judgment.

 I now come to the glorious epocha of the

reign of Philip II. I shall impartially examine those facts which history presents to me, without the least fear of being charged with a malicious spirit, if my reflections should, in some measure, diminish the general idea of that conquest, which was obtained by such an easy entrance into Portugal. The Spaniards, and the Duke of Alba, who led them on, possess so many trophies, acquired with toil and glory, that it is not necessary to mention a doubtful victory. I shall, however, take care to cite only Spanish authors, and draw from Spain itself a part of my critical reflections.

After the death of that rash King, Don Sebastian, in Africa, with the flower of the Portuguese nation, the succession was for some time held by his aged uncle, the Cardinal Don Henry. Three claimants, even before the face of this weak and decrepit monarch, engaged in disputes for the spoils he should leave behind him. The Duchess of Bragança, with some right, but no power; Philip II. with both right and power, and Don Antonio, Prior of Crato, without either one or the other. The death of the cardinal monarch, precipitated by the chagrin which had been occasioned by the ambition of his heirs, was the fatal prognostic of a civil war. Philip, supported by an army composed of the best troops in Europe, and commanded by the Duke of Alba, produced an acknowledgment of his rights in a will of the late King, Don Henry; for which he was indebted to the contrivance of Christopher de Mora, his confidential secretary. The Duchess of Bragança gave up all her pretensions; while Don Antonio, equally weak and rash, obstinately refused all the offers of Philip, and had the audacity to have recourse to arms.

The Portuguese nation, dispirited by the loss of Don Sebastian and all his nobility, did not possess the means of re-establishing itself during the short and tumultuous reign of the incapacitated and timorous Don Henry. The kingdom had neither a fleet, nor arms, nor money; and the people were divided. Prudence suggested it would be impolitic to irritate Philip II. while the spirit of national hatred revolted at the idea of submitting to the Castilian government. Three out of the five governors, were resolved not to obstruct the entrance of Don Philip into the kingdom. The hatred of the people of Lisbon against the Spaniards, was the sole motive which engaged them to favour the Prior of Crato, and to proclaim him king. Four of the governors fled to the frontiers of Spain, where they confirmed the rights of Philip II. John Telles alone, being undetermined with which party to act, became odious to both, and was driven from his government.

While all this was passing, the Duke of Alba entered Portugal with a considerable army: according to Ferreiras, it consisted of 30,000 men; but if we are to credit Cabrera and Osorio, it did not amount to above half that number. Elvas sent its keys as far as Llerena; Villa Viçosa was taken possession of without any effusion of blood, by the conspiracy of a Castilian soldier. Don John de Azevedo, admiral of Portugal, who was shut up in Estremoz, after much threats and bravado, shamefully surrendered on the first cannon-shot. Such were the first events of the war. From Alemtejo, the Spaniards marched to Setuval, which submitted without resistance: the castle of Outaō was the only post which occasioned a small effusion of blood. After having made himself master of these places with so little difficulty, the duke embarked on board a very powerful fleet, which coasted along Portugal from Cadiz, and commanded the seas. He then disembarked his troops at

Cascaes, without opposition from Don Diego de Meneses, who was an enemy to both parties, and marched directly to Lisbon.

The new King Don Antonio, without foreign succours, without money, and without the confidence of his subjects, got together an army, composed of the lowest and most incapable part of the people of Lisbon, and entrenched himself at Belem, two miles from that city where his position was forced, and his troops overcome without much trouble, in the only battle or onset which took place in this war. He fled by Sacavem, and took refuge at Coimbra, where he obtained a reinforcement of troops, and was a second time beaten by Don Sancho d'Avila, at Aveiro. From thence he embarked at Oporto for the Terceiras (Açores,) or Cape Verd Islands, where he sustained, for some time, this unfortunate contest; till at length he determined to abandon his desperate pretensions, and to pass the rest of his life as a private person in France, where he died.

This war lasted from June 19, when the Spaniards entered Portugal, to the end of August. The promptitude of its success proves the facility with which it was carried on, and the little resistance it met with. The line of

H

march adopted by the Duke d'Alba was the best, from the circumstance of his having a fleet ready to transport his troops to Cascaes. But that general did not succeed in finishing the war, nor did he take sufficient precautions to attain its object, since Don Antonio found the means to escape and re-appear at the head of 12,000 men. Nay, if this prince had been fortunately joined at that time by the Marshal Philip Strozzi, who afterwards fought for him at the Terceiras, Fortune perhaps might have turned her back on the conqueror. This mistake has not escaped the observation of the Spanish historians.

The error of having let the Prior of Crato escape, was the natural consequence of the plan laid down for the conquest of Portugal. the rapid reduction of the different places in Alemtejo, determined the operations on that side, as the most easy of access; but if the Duke d'Alba had left these places for the present, which, whether taken or not, would have had no effect on his final success before Lisbon, and had cut off the passage of the provinces from Don Antonio, in passing by Abrantes and Santarem, which would have shut him up in the corner of Lisbon, there cannot be the least doubt that he would have finished the war at one stroke; and that Don Antonio, not being able to escape either by sea or land, must have accepted the propositions which were made to him, or have fallen the victim of his rashness.

The war of the rebellion of Portugal will furnish me with additional examples. After having suffered, during sixty years, the Spanish yoke, the Portuguese, availing themselves of the security and weakness of the government of Philip IV. proclaimed Don Juan de Bragança; who, without his knowledge, and without having made any noble efforts to merit such an elevation, was placed upon the throne. This revolution was completed even with less difficulty and effusion of blood, than the conquest of the Duke d'Alba. Every one is acquainted with this point of history, which has been rendered so interesting by the style of Abbé Vertot.* The war which succeeded to the revolution lasted twenty-eight years, with great loss to the Spaniards. But as the events of it bear a great resemblance to each other, and

* In a small volume 12mo, called *Revolutions de Portugal*; it is considered as one of the classical books of the French. T.

were none of them decisive; I shall confine my reflections to three epochas, which will give a sufficient knowledge of the military faults committed in it, and of those inevitable misfortunes that arise from the pursuit of a false system.

The first years of this war did not produce any events worthy of being recorded; because the court of Madrid, embarrassed with other more important contests, particularly those of France and Catalonia, could give very little attention to this; while Portugal, instead of profiting from such neglect, gave itself up to supineness and indolence, without making any preparations for the war that threatened it.

In 1658, Don Louis de Haro, a good minister, but a bad general, took upon him the command of the troops in Estremadura. He entered with a powerful army into Alemtejo, and undertook the siege of Elvas. After much time had been lost before this place, the Portuguese army arrived to succour it, January 14, 1659, when Don Louis, after having his lines forced, fled to Badajoz, leaving 6000 men dead on the field of battle, and 1000 prisoners, among whom were four grandees of Spain, together with the artillery, baggage, and military chest, the standard of Charles V. and the strong-box of the general, which contained papers of great importance.

In 1661, Don Juan of Austria, son of Philip IV. took upon him the command of the army, in the place of Don Louis de Haro, who was more usefully occupied in negotiating the peace of the Pyrenees. This prince, following the same methodical system, abandoned the trunk to lop off the branches. Finding the siege of Elvas too difficult an undertaking, Don Juan passed two years in taking and fortifying certain inconsiderable places, as Arronches, Olivença, and Xerumena; and having ventured into Alemtejo, he got possession of Estremoz and the whole province, and pushed into Estremadura as far as Alcaçer do Sal; but after a campaign of two months he was forced to retire, on account of the havock that was beginning to be made in his army by disease and famine. He was beaten twice in his retreat; at Ameixial and Estremoz, and he finished his campaign with the diminution of his military character, and two-thirds of his army. The battle of Estremoz took place, June 8, 1663. The Portuguese were commanded by the Count Schomberg, and supported by the English and

French, who performed prodigies of valour. The Spaniards fought with the courage attributed to the troops of Charles V.; but they could not resist the ardour and despair of their enemies. Don Juan had two horses shot under him, and acted with great skill and resolution; but Schomberg proved superior to the prince, and was the saviour of Portugal. The loss of the Spaniards amounted to 12,000 men killed and taken prisoners.

The last entrance of the Spaniards into Portugal, was that of the Marquis of Caracena, with a powerful army. This general, who was possessed of great talents and much experience, followed the stream, or rather the orders of the court; and in compliance with the old system, sought misfortune in the plains of Alemtejo, where he lost, June 17, 1664, the battle of Villa Viçosa. It was to the ability of Schomberg, and the valour of the French, that the Portuguese were indebted for this victory, which completed the disgrace of Spain, brought on peace, and took from the Spaniards all desire of returning to similar encounters. Ten thousand Spaniards left on the field of battle; 4000 prisoners, and all the artillery, baggage, and standards, testified the complete triumph of the

Portuguese. The sensibility of Philip IV. surpassed, after this battle, all that he had felt during a long and unfortunate reign. He could not console himself for having been conquered by an handful of rebels, as he was pleased to call the Portuguese. Charles II. his successor, made peace, because it was impossible for him to continue the war. If it had continued throughout a century, it could not have had any other conclusion, while the manner of carrying it on was obstinately adhered to. This is evident, because the ill success of the several campaigns could not be attributed to the generals, Don Juan of Austria, the Marquis of Caracena, the Count of St. Germain, and the Duke d'Ossona, who had distinguished themselves in far more important wars; nor to the weakness of the army; for in no time were the Spaniards more warlike, than from the age of Charles V. to the end of the reign of Philip IV. nor to the skill or activity of the Portuguese; for except Count Schomberg, whom they hated as a foreigner, incapacity, presumption, and discord, were the leading features of the Portuguese army.

The sole foundation of these misfortune was the uncertainty, the indiscretion, and the want of system in carrying on this war. On reading its history, it appears to partake of something of the ancient spirit of knight errantry; and that prince tacitly agreed, that such a province should be the theatre of war, where armies might assemble as at a tournament, and decide, as in lists, contests very different from those of knighthood. Every General departed from his object, became embarrassed in fruitless or dangerous enterprises, and conducted himself contrary to every principle of art or reason.

This error has been discovered in our age, but no pains have been employed to find a remedy; for, notwithstanding many favourable opportunities have presented themselves, the means of carrying on this war have never been investigated but at the moment of its renewal. Maps have not been formed, nor the roads, mountains, and rivers, reconnoitered. Military plans have not been accepted, or even proposed, when peace afforded the best opportunity for those investigations. No arrangements have been made respecting the subsistence and equipment of troops, the construction or maintenance of bridges, the different kinds of arms, and the mode of employing them. No new system has been admitted in the place of the ancient one, which the court of Spain has rejected with disdain.

The war for the Spanish succession does not offer a subject for reflection; because, except some inroads, fortunately executed by the Marquis de Bey, the war has been purely defensive on the side of Spain. In the last war, a very different plan has been proposed, but it did not succeed. The disgrace of Spain is recent, and inspires the most profound reflections. Experience should be the fruit of misfortune.

We live in an enlightened age. War is the science of sovereigns. Systems are calculated and projects are verified. The great Frederick has given lessons to future ages. According to his system, rivers form the most natural conductors to enter a kingdom, whether to attack or defend it; their course directs the plans that must be formed for action or for subsistence. Such is the fundamental principle of those wars which he has terminated with so much glory. The most advantageous consequences must ever flow from such a solid and immoveable basis of military operation.

BOOK IV.

NATIONAL CHARACTER AND GOVERNMENT.

CHAPTER I.

MANNERS OF THE PORTUGUESE; THE FIDALGOS; WOMEN; PUBLIC AMUSEMENTS, DANCES, BULL-FEASTS, &c.

THE character of the Portuguese bears a strong resemblance to that of the Spaniards; they possess the same disposition to idleness and superstition, the same kind of courage, the same pride, but more politeness and deceit, which arises from the rigour of their present government; the same national zeal, and, above all, a decided spirit of independence, which incites the most violent hatred towards the Spaniards, who have been their tyrants, and the English, who are their masters.

The manners of the northern provinces of Portugal have a positive resemblance to those of Scotland. Their inhabitants are a fine race of men, free, sincere, brave, full of prejudices of national hatred and patriotic love. They are universally hospitable, and, in the provinces of Entre Minho e Douro and Traz os Montes, there are no inns. In the south, on the contrary, and, above all, at Lisbon, the inhabitants are robbers, misers, traitors, brutal, fierce, and morose, with an external appearance which bears all the characters of their detestable natures. Some exceptions, however, are to be met with, particularly among the nobility; whose birth is superior to that of the Spanish nobles, and who possess more affable manners, as well as a more communicative spirit, which indeed they derive from a more frequent intercourse with foreigners.

The Portuguese possess an innate enmity to the English and the Spaniards. The French nation is that with which they sympathize the most; of which they entertain the greatest apprehension, and for which they bear the highest respect. They are governed by a prejudice, that no place can resist the attack of French besiegers. This sympathy, as well as its concomitant opinion, are both beneficial, and proceed from the gaiety, the vivacity, the inconstancy, and turn of mind common to these two people; a relation which able politicians may employ to their mutual interest. In politics, the knowledge of national character is not always sufficiently considered; the interests of sovereigns are alone regarded; and it often happens, that the most important negotiations fail, from an ignorance in the art of reconciling the contrarieties of these high interests, and the characters of nations.

The Fidalgos or grandees of Portugal are not so ill informed as those of Spain; but they are almost as incommunicative, as haughty, and are more jealous of their women. Very few of them enter into the army, because they cannot obtain permission. They have carried audacity, tyranny, and independence to the highest pitch, from the epocha of the proclamation of Don Juan de Bragança, in 1640, to the assassination of the king in 1756. The Count d'Oeyras availed himself of the latter event to reduce and lower them in a much greater degree than they had ever been elevated. He restored the authority of the king and the laws amid streams of blood. The greater part of the principal persons among them perished in prison. These Fidalgos which frequent the court are poor, base, and grovelling;

those alone who are particularly attached to him are permitted to serve in the army; or such who have not any quality that can give him umbrage. The rest of the nobility live without credit; at once ignorant, loaded with debts, and without any exterior distinction.

The Portuguese women possess the finest colour of any in Europe, the finest teeth, and the most beautiful hair. Their dress, though it bears some resemblance to the dress of the Turkish ladies, does not set them off to advantage; as the lacing themselves too close enlarges their bosoms. Their shoes are very high and large, so that almost all of them have big feet, and walk ill; they therefore seldom walk. They are otherwise gallant, witty, and well informed; but they live in a rigorous state of solitude. Intrigue is not only difficult but dangerous in Portugal. The women are never seen but at the churches and places of diversion. They are very cleanly and coquettish. The boxes of the theatres are highly decorated by the presence of these charming females; but the small portion of liberty which they possess obliges the men, and particularly foreigners, to consider them in no other point of view, than as beautiful portraits arranged for the decoration of a gallery. Women of the common rank suffer an almost equal degree of restraint: many of them are very handsome, and however poor they may be, they pay a very particular attention to the arrangement of their hair and the dress of the head, which they always keep uncovered, even in the streets.

The Portuguese theatre is worse and in a lower style than that of Spain: their pieces are all in the burlésque, like the Italian pantalonades, but with less wit and more buffoonery. They have neither an equal variety nor so fine a dramatic collection as has been furnished by Lopez de Vega, Calderone, Moreto, &c. Not one good writer has employed himself in the service of the Portuguese theatre, but Camoens, who has given a good translation of Amphytrion, which is never performed; and Ferreira, who composed a very good tragedy called Ines de Castro, after the Greek model. At present they translate from the French and Italian theatre, but the bad taste of the country and the harshness of the language* destroys the

---

* The Portuguese language has long preserved the Latin tongue, though much corrupted; and several Portuguese compositions yet extant are as good Latin

merit of them. The actors are bad, but well dressed. Their dances and music are excellent, and give some little life to the two theatres of Lisbon. They have very good Italian operas,

as any monk of the twelfth century would have wrote: the following verses, in honour of St. Ursula and her eleven thousand virgins, will give a specimen of this affinity:—

> *Canto tuas palmas, famosos canto triumphos,*
> *Ursula, divinos martyr concede favores;*
> *Subjectas sacra nympha, feros animosa tyrannos,*
> *Tu phœnix, vivendo ardes, ardendo triumphas.*
> *Illustres generosa choros das Ursula bellos;*
> *Das rosa bellas rosas, fortes das sancta columnas;*
> *Æternos vivas annos, o regia planta!*
> *Devotos cantando hymnos, invoco favores.*
> *Tam puras nymphas amo, adoro, canto, celebro*
> *Per vos felices annos, o candida turba,*
> *Per vos innumeros de Christo spero favores.*

The affinity of the Portuguese with the Latin does not destroy the assertion of the author; when it is spoken sweetness is found in the expression, but an uncouth harshness generally offends the ear of the stranger; and this is attributed chiefly to the vast number of diphthongs, which are no less than sixteen in that language. Another great defect of the language itself is, the difficulty, or rather the impossibility, of making a true distinction betwixt the three tenses of the verbs; that is, the preter-imperfect, the preter-perfect, and the future. T.

and that of the king is one of the best composed in Europe.

The Portuguese are by no means of a communicative disposition, and there is but little society among them, particularly at Lisbon. The government, which is become naturally suspicious, since the horrid plot against the king, has prohibited all assemblies; which regulation accords wonderfully with the extreme jealousy of the nation; so that Lisbon is without diversions. There are occasional balls; but they are principally for the amusement of strangers. The national dance is called the Foffa; it is danced in couples, like the Spanish Fandango, to the tinkling of a bad guitar. Its motions are extremely indecent, and the dancer generally accompanies his gesticulation with expressions equally ludicrous and obscene.

There are bull-feasts in Portugal as well as in Spain, where, notwithstanding every precaution to prevent mischief, accidents sometimes happen from the very great awkwardness of the combatants. But the most singular circumstance belonging to these feasts is, that permission is given to persons of the first rank to engage in these spectacles, under the cover of a mask, and that some of them always avail themselves of this privilege. They always engage on horseback with small lances, called in Spain Rejones. If the horseman loses his stirrup, if his hat falls, or if he is thrown into disorder, he is obliged to dismount and to revenge himself on foot, and to fight the bull alone; not like the Spaniards behind a cloak, but face to face, with a sabre. The bulls of Portugal, however, are not equal to those of spain, either for strength, or size, or fierceness; and they have a ball fixed on the top of each horn; so that the bull-feasts of Portugal are less cruel, as well as dangerous, than those of Spain.

CHAPTER II.

DRESS, BUILDINGS, POLICE, CLIMATE, EARTHQUAKES, COUNTRY HOUSES, &c.

Having described the dress of the women, it remains only to speak of that of the men, which is that of other European nations, cut short, and accompanied with a Spanish cloak and a long sword. Their clothes are ill made, very dirty, and have a Jewish appearance, which by no means set off the Portuguese countenance. Those who belong to the court almost universally wear uniforms.

The houses also are very dirty, ill built, and inconvenient; gnats, bugs, and insects of every kind, bred amid the filth of Lisbon, make its residence insupportable; while the slightness of the roofs and walls are incapable of protecting the inhabitants from the rigour of the winter and the north wind. Since the great earthquake, it has not been thought prudent to construct solid buildings. The king himself lives in a kind of barrack. These barracks are made in Holland, and brought by sea from thence in a state to be immediately erected. This iseffected by putting all the different parts together, and consolidating them with a coat of plaster. These houses may be built or removed in twenty-four hours.

The streets of all the towns are full of every kind of filth, without any lights, but such as glimmer before the statues of the Virgin Mary; they are therefore by no means safe after it is dark, and are also infested by all the dogs of the place, who always pass the night in the streets; but, besides their continual barking, it is astonishing that no accident happens from these hungry animals; one of whom, if seized with madness, would, in the course of two or three hours, spread that fatal calamity through every quarter of the city. The number of dogs in Lisbon, who are the nocturnal inhabitants of the streets, are supposed to amount to 80,000. About eight o'clock in the winter evenings, all the shopkeepers and common people place themselves on the thresholds of their doors, to chant the rosary. This noise lasts about an hour, after which time the streets overflow with robbers, chamber-pots, dogs, and officers of justice. The latter proceed in bands of fifteen or twenty persons, armed with long swords, which they present to the passengers, whom they surround and interrogate. This troop, which belongs to the police, is neither feared by thieves, nor held in estimation by the government, which employs, in Lisbon, patroles from the garrison, that consists of from 4 to 5000 men. A part of the common disturbances is caused by the Negroes and Mulattoes, of which there are supposed to be in Lisbon so many as 150,000; by the misery of the people, and the facility of finding hiding places in the subsisting ruins of this unfortunate city, of which a description is given in a future part of this volume.

The climate is temperate, and refreshed in the hottest seasons by a sea breeze, which purifies the air and renders it wholesome. It rains in deluges during five months of the year, when the lower streets of the city become impassable, from the torrents which descend from the upper parts. In the seven dry months there are frequent hurricanes, which raise such thick clouds of dust as to obscure the sky. Earthquakes are so frequent, that a year seldom passes without two or three slight shocks; and the bituminous vapours which rise upon the Tagus, prove that beneath it and within the mountains of Lisbon and its environs, igneous matter is in a continual agitation, whose active powers occasion loud explosions, and violent periodical shocks. The earthquake in 1755 was preceded, 150 years before, by one attended with similar effects; and that by several others, during a thousand preceding years, in the same proportion.

There are no public walks in this city or its environs, but they are adorned with country houses, some of which are maintained in a good style. It is in these retreats that good company is to be found; that is to say, the foreign merchants; who alone are in a condition to sustain the expence, and to enjoy the pleasures of them.

CHAPTER III.

JUSTICE, PRISONS, TRIBUNALS, COUNCILS, CITIES, ORDERS, ARCHBISHOPRICS, BISHOPRICS, THE PATRIARCH, RELIGION, THE INQUISITION, THE EXPULSION OF THE JESUITS, SCHISM OF PORTUGAL, &c.

The police of Lisbon, and indeed of all Portugal, bad as it is, is in the hands of judges, named Juiz de Fora, who are subordinate to the corregedors and ouvidors, the whole kingdom being divided into corregedorias and ouvidorias. Nothing can exceed the insolence and cupidity of this great number of different judges. Justice is administered with the same extortions, the same miserable chicane, and the same load of pleadings as in Spain; that is to say, much worse than in any other part of Europe.

The prisons are the abodes of barbarity and despair. The innocent return from them entirely ruined, and the guilty pardoned, and in an equal state of wretchedness. Impunity never fails to produce crimes. I myself saw at Lisbon a servant assassinate his comrade at noon-day, in the middle of the street, and retire with great calmness from the scene, with the knife in his hand, to be conducted to prison, which he entered smiling; and from which, after some months, he was permitted to depart, in order to perform the office of public executioner. The Limoero is the public prison of Lisbon, and generally inhabited by 4 or 5000 unfortunate persons. State criminals, nobles, officers of every rank, whether for slight or heavy offences, debtors, and foreigners, are mingled together, without any distinction of rank or treatment, but as they can afford to pay the jailer. The rich who are committed to prison are ruined by its extortions, and the poor have no dependence but public charity; for the king makes no allowance for them; and hence it is that such numbers are imprisoned, and for such trifling causes. There are also secret state prisons, the abodes of torture and despair, horrible dungeons, beneath the towers of St. Vincent, St. Julian, and Bugio; in which languish, in despair and darkness, many nobles and heads of the first families, the tardy but irrevocable victims of policy, of justice, and of despotism. The continual disappearance of well-known persons creates frequent alarm and consternation throughout Lisbon and Portugal; of which I cannot give a more faithful picture than Narbal presents to Telemachus, of the state of Tyre under the government of the tyrant Pygmalion.

The criminal chief justice is the Archbishop of Evora Saldanha, the intimate friend of the Count d'Oeyras, possessing the same kind of disposition, and the most wealthy ecclesiastic of the kingdom. He has a great share of power, and is fond of pomp.

The first tribunal is that of justice, named the Desembargo do Paço, or the Parliament,* and consists of two divisions. That of Lisbon has the sole right of final judgment; while that of Oporto is subject to its revision. This parliament was established in the beginning of the fifteenth century, by John I. The number of counsellors, named Desembargadors, is not fixed. That of Lisbon has the jurisdiction of Algarve, Alemtejo, Estremadura, and of the district of Castel-Branco, and Riba de Coa. That of Oporto extends over Traz os Montes, Entre Minho e Douro, and Beira. Each parliament is divided into two chambers; that of

---

* Rather the privy council. T.

supplication, which consists of thirty-nine counsellors, and that of civil justice, which consists of twenty-four. The rest are merely honorary.

The Council of State established in 1557, by the Queen Regent Catherine, during the minority of Don Sebastian, is composed of four ecclesiastical counsellors, five seculars, and a secretary of state, who is commonly the king's minister. Its department regards the archbishoprics, bishoprics, capitanias, governments, vice-royalties, embassies, alliances and marriages.

The Council of War is composed of four counsellors, and a secretary, who is, generally, the minister of the war department. At present it is filled by Don Louis d'Acunha. On very pressing occasions it is united to the council of state.

The Council of Finance is divided into fifteen tribunals, viz. of accounts, customs, the Indies, mines, magazines, Madeira, the mint, the fleet, &c. This council consists of three departments, that of the kingdom, that of Africa, and that of the Indies and the fleets.

The office of Secretary of State, was reformed by John IV. It is divided into two parts, which Count d'Oeyras has united in his own person. That of signatures, whose business it is to prepare for the sign manual of the king, all those papers or ordinances which issue from him respecting all the branches of government, except such as regard the second division, viz. that of favours and rewards, which pass alone through the hands of this secretary. The title of *Secretario das merces e graças* is the only one which the Count d'Oeyras assumes: he lets others take the titles and exercise the duties of the remaining branches, reserving to himself, however, their power and emoluments.

Besides these tribunals, the Cortes or states of the kingdom, are assembled, on pressing occasions, to make alterations in the laws or political constitution; or to introduce new arrangements in the finances or the government. But as this overlooking and powerful tribunal cannot be pleasing to the king or his ministers, it is but seldom summoned to its duties.

There are three Orders in Portugal, from which the king, as grandmaster, derives a revenue of 2,000,000 of crusades.* The order

* About £100,000.

of Christ, instituted by King Denis, in 1319, ceased to be in estimation with the wars against the Moors; and it is debased by a most foolish and misplaced pride, which has introduced into it a species of knights from among the lowest class of the people. It has long been, and still continues to be, a prevailing vanity among the Fidalgos or nobles, that the valets behind their coaches, or who serve them at table, should be decorated with an order of knighthood. Hence it is, that those orders, adorning alike the persons of the king, the princes, the nobles, and their lackeys, are all of them, but especially that of Christ, considered with contempt in Portugal. This order possesses the grand priory of Thomar, 454 commandries, and a revenue of near £50,000 sterling. The order of St. James, separated from that of Spain, since the year 1290, has the grand priory of Palmela, 150 commandries, and a revenue of near £30,000. The order of Avis, established at Evora, but subject to that of Calatrava, was transferred to Avis in 1161. It has the grand priory of Avis, fifty commandries, and upwards of £20,000 per annum. These orders were founded in times of anarchy, by the fanaticism and brutality of Christian knights. They sustained themselves for a long time, by their united strength and courage; and above all, by the opposition of the Moors (whose hostile spirit never abated) which rendered them necessary to Christian princes. That of Calatrava was established by two monks, who were better soldiers than priests. That of St. James owed its institution to a famous robber, named Fernandes, who to obtain heaven devoted all his iniquities to God, and employed against the Infidels, his robberies, his courage, and his cruelty. But in a short time the great acquisitions which these knights made from the Moors, rendered them not only insolent, but formidable, to their own sovereigns. They made alliances with foreign enemies, ravaged the kingdom, and joined tyranny to independance. More than once the grandmasters have allied themselves to the Moorish kings, led the Infidel troops into their own country, and assisted them in laying waste the Christian states. The kings of Portugal, following the example of other European sovereigns, found the only means of putting an end to this abuse of power in ceasing to confide the charge of grandmaster to subjects.

Besides these three orders, that of St. John or of Malta, has twenty-five commandries, and a revenue of about £30,000. In Spain and Portugal, the cross of Malta is taken up and laid down, without the least ceremony; and the Portuguese frequently wear it from mére fancy, without having any connection whatever with the order whose symbol it is.

There are in Portugal eighteen cities, of which Bragança, Beja, Lagos, Silves, and Tavira are not episcopal sees: three archbishoprics, Lisbon, subject to the Patriarch, Evora, which is worth upwards of 80,000 crusades* per annum; and Braga, which is possessed by an illegitimate brother of the king's, who dares not come to Lisbon from the fear of being imprisoned. This is the situation also of two other natural brothers. There are ten bishoprics; Porto, Miranda, Coimbra, Guarda, Lamego, Viseu, Leiria, Elvas, Portalegre and Faro. In Asia there are three archbishoprics; Goa, which has the primacy of the east, Da Serra and Cranganore; and four bishoprics, Cochin, Malacca, Meliapour, and Macao. The three first are *in partibus*. In America, there is one archbishopric, La Bahia; and four bishoprics, Rio Janeiro, Pernambucco, Maranham,

---

* About £100,000.

and the great Para. In Africa, there is one archbishopric, Funchal, in the island of Madeira; and four bishoprics, Angola, St. Thomas, Cabo Verde, and Angra.

The clergy of Portugal is much too powerful, and far too numerous for the general population. The monks, nuns, and priests amount to more than 200,000, in a country which contains but 2,000,000 inhabitants. Hence it is, that the Count d'Oeyras has made an arrangement for their diminution; especially the nuns, by extinguishing one half of their convents, and prohibiting all the religious orders, whether male or female, to receive any novice within the age of twenty-five years, and without an express permission from the king. The Portuguese clergy is equally ignorant and dissolute: the liberty and the power attached to this order of men, occasion the most public profanation of its character. That scandalous conduct, which lessens the veneration of the people, is more injurious to religion than the continual railleries of the English, the introduction of philosophical books, and the quarrels with the court of Rome. The monks live in the most unrestrained licentiousness; and the nuns have been, to the present time, little better than cloistered prostitutes. All the convents follow the example of that of Odivelas, where 300 beautiful and coquettish nuns formed a seraglio for John V. which has been the hot-bed of royal illegitimate children; and where, besides, each of these religious ladies had her particular lovers. Throwing aside their professional habits, covered with rouge, with patches, and diamonds, they excited and practised the most refined gallantry, and passed for the most attractive favourites of the Portuguese nobility. This scandal to religion has induced the Count d'Oeyras to diminish the number of convents, and to restrain them by very austere regulations. The evil, however, is not entirely rooted out, and the clergy of Portugal, with the religious orders, both male and female, may be considered as the most licentious and the most abandoned in the Christian world.

At the head of the clergy is the Patriarch, the primate of Portugal, and the director of the church. This dignity was first established at the beginning of the present century, on the intercession of John V. who expended a large sum of money to obtain this favour. It will one day, perhaps, be very prejudicial to the court of Rome, by producing a schism, which is already freely spoke of, and which the court of London will support with all its power. The patriarch wears the same robes as the pope, when he officiates at the altar; and the canons of the patriarchal church appear in the dress of cardinals.

The Inquisition is very moderate in Portugal; it is rather a tribunal of police, than of fire and flames, which it formerly was. Its sentences are directed to the lower classes of the people; to monks or priests who are guilty of heresy from ignorance, and sustain it from fanaticism; impostors who pretend to practise sorcery, and Jews of the lowest class who are so weak as to boast of their religion. The *auto da fé* which I saw in the beginning of the year 1766, was composed of about forty shameless wretches, who would have deserved the whip in any country. No one was committed to the flames; and unless that happens, the scene is not interesting to the Portuguese. The punishments were proportioned to their crimes, and by no means violent; the greater part of the criminals were whipped, or sent into exile. Those which were objects of pity, were two or three priests and a lawyer, who had spoken ill of the holy tribunal; these were condemned to a perpetual imprisonment in the dungeons of their enemies, who never fail to be zealous avengers of their own wrongs.

The heat of the climate, and the natural warmth of their constitutions, with their ignorance and indolence, render the Portuguese very bad Christians. Carnal inclinations are those which they know not how to resist, and therefore endeavour to supply the place of morality with every kind of superstition. There is no catholic country whatever, in which a more superstitious devotion is paid to saints, relics, miracles, and other religious mummeries; because no people stand more in need of expiations for their low and filthy debaucheries, and for the avarice and revengeful spirit which continually agitates the soul of a Portuguese. The national worship is equally divided between God and the Virgin Mary; and since the alliance of this nation with England, St. George is become a principal object of their devout attentions. Once a year, his equestrian statue, armed at all points, and covered with all the jewels of the crown, is carried in solemn procession. The more the Portuguese deviate from the duties of the Gospel, the more they attach themselves to the exterior circumstances of religion. Hence it is, that the Count d'Oeyras proceeds with the greatest precaution in those projects which he has already begun, in opposition to the power of the court of Rome.

The first of his operations was the expulsion of the Jesuits. That singular order of men was all-powerful in Spain and Portugal; for, abandoning the common people to the monks, they reserved to themselves the task of directing the consciences of the great, of ministers, and of kings.

The order of the Jesuits is a political association of spiritual and ambitious men, bound together by one strong and common interest. Implicit obedience to their head, is the basis of their actions: all their views, designs, and operations tend to the same end, and proceed from the same principle; no personal interest, no division exists among them. This order is the image of a perfect republic, and consequently is contrary to all other governments. A Jesuit is a citizen only of his own order, is a natural enemy of every society, and according to the principles of good policy, is not admissible into any well ordered state. It is astonishing that such a body of men should have been received under any government; nevertheless, it has insinuated itself under the cloak of religion into many. The arts, the sciences, and the education of youth, were the means by which it acquired all its distinctions. Many states, however, not dazzled by their real and useful qualifications, adopted a more enlarged way of thinking, than those who received them. These austere and learned philosophers, who consecrated themselves to the office of enlightening nations, occupied themselves also in politics, in commerce, and in war; more skilful even in intrigue than in science, and always contriving to manage the leading interests of mankind, they were suspected of employing the most Machiavelian and criminal means to obtain their objects: they have been accused of lighting up funeral piles, preparing poisons, sharpening poniards, and arming fanaticism! Several sovereigns have at length opened their eyes, and discovered their ambition. The parliaments in France, the senate of Venice, the suspicious apprehensions of Carvalho, the revolt of Madrid, have driven them successively from France, Venice, Portugal, and Spain. In a political view every country is justified in having employed the most violent means to extirpate this society; but morally speaking, they have been treated with great injustice, particularly in Spain and Portugal.

An affair of the greatest importance had almost entirely ruined them with these two courts; and by depriving them of the character of confessors to the kings and their ministers, destroyed the basis of their power. The Marquis of Carvajal, favourite of Ferdinand VI. King of Spain, who without the title of Minister directed the government of that country, had been gained over by the Queen Barbara, who was an Infanta of Portugal. The known state of the king, her husband's, constitution; and her own attachment to Farinelli, the famous Italian singer, leaving her without hopes of children, she had directed all her tenderness, her wishes, her cares, and her intrigues, towards her country. Mr. Keene, the English ambassador, who enjoyed all her confidence, had traced out to her, conjointly with the Portuguese minister, the Duke of Alba, and some others, the plan of a treaty very advantageous to Portugal, and still more so to England. The Marquis of Carvajal, joined with the queen in advancing its success, intoxicated by his affinity to the house of Bragança, of which the court of Lisbon made a great parade.

The object of this treaty was an exchange of the colony of St. Sacrement upon the river La Plata, for the settlements on the river San Pedro and some others, which by surrounding Brasil, would bring together the Portuguese frontiers, would extend them along the great Cordilleras, and the rivers which flow from them, and multiply in a great degree the means of securing a smuggling intercourse with the richest provinces of Spain. Nevertheless, the pretext for making this exchange, was to abolish the contraband trade of the colony of St. Sacrement. The opposition of the Marquis de l'Ensenada, minister for foreign affairs, of the marine and the Indies, was attributed to his partizans, the Jesuits, and suspended for two years the exchanging the ratifications of this treaty. That minister absolutely refused his signature. He was accordingly stripped of his employments, and exiled to Grenada, while those monks which were most violent against the Jesuits, were appointed confessors to the king, the queen, and the royal family. It was at this time that the fable of their kingdom in

Paraguay began to gain credit, and which occasioned a miserable publication, with the title of Nicolas I. The origin of this fable is as follows.

Paraguay is an immense portion of South America, which extends from the capitania of St. Vincent in Brasil, to the left bank of Rio de la Plata, runs up behind Chili and Peru to the unknown country of the Amazons, and has no fixed limits. This vast country is watered by noble rivers, whose banks were peopled by various savage nations, till the division of South America was made by Spain and Portugal, who alone have any settlements in it. The two courts of Madrid and Lisbon, after a long succession of disputes relative to the limits, not being able to come to any positive determination respecting this country, which no one yet had penetrated,* and being alarmed with mutual fears respecting mutual encroachments; the Spaniards fearing for Peru, and the Portuguese for Brasil; they united in manifesting their confidence in these

---

* The limits have been fixed since by Spanish and Portuguese commissaries, sent for that purpose from the two kingdoms. T.

good fathers, whose indefatigable zeal in propagating the Gospel, appeared to merit such a recompence. They mutually agreed, therefore, to concede this immense country to the society of Jesuits, with an exact demarkation only of its breadth, as its length has never been discovered.

The Jesuits, superior to the rest of mankind in the art of persuasion, and labouring for themselves, made an incredible progress in their designs. At the end of fifty years, and to the disgrace of the other colonies, the country of the missionaries was filled with villages, the catholic faith was triumphant, and the savages civilized, happy, and subject to the wisest of governments. No people on earth were more contented, labour and property was all in common. There were neither rich nor poor, nor dignities, nor great, nor little; there was no inequality whatever; and consequently neither avarice, ambition, or jealousy: every one contributed equally his portion of labour, and received an equal retribution from it. Every village was one numerous family, of which the Jesuit was the father; and the society itself was the mother of this happy republic.

The power of these reverend fathers, by a

system of politics very different from the greater part of human governments, was founded upon a perfect union of public utility with individual happiness.

This wonderful republic existed in peace. The Jesuits, from their moderate spirit, and to avoid all appearance of ostentation, payed the kings of Spain and Portugal certain small tribute, without murmuring at the unjustifiable power which required them of a free people, who, united in a society of their own establishment, could not be reasonably considered either as subjects to the Spaniards or Portuguese. It was not long, however, before the two courts, jealous of the progress of such a population, agreed to divide between them the fruits of the labours of the Jesuits. The latter represented in vain that their rights were legitimated by the concession of the country, as well as the injustice of doing violence to a free people; who, on embracing the catholic religion, and adopting the European manners, did not propose to give themselves masters. These remonstrances were treated as criminal and treasonable by Spaniards and Portuguese, who entered with arms in their hands into these colonies. The Indians exerted themselves to the utmost in their defence; but overcome by the superior discipline of European soldiers, a small number of them received the yoke, while the rest established themselves further up the country, taking the fathers with them to console them in their distress, and protesting against the tyranny and injustice of the barbarians of Europe.

The Jesuits now found themselves in a very perplexed situation; threatened, in Europe, with persecution and exile; prohibited from continuing their missions; while they must have been highly unjust to their proselytes, if they had advised them to give up their liberty; their sagacity was often disconcerted. At length, however, an accidental discovery was made of their Machiavelian system, and at once exposed their conduct.

A captain of Spanish dragoons, who was a native of France, the Chevalier de Bonneval, found in a village of the mission of Parana, where he commanded after the conquest, the instructions of the order, addressed to the principal Jesuit of the district. He himself repeated to me the three following articles. 1st. " If the bishop of Buenos Ayres, or any other " ecclesiastical officer should come to make a " pastoral visit, and to interfere in the affairs

"of the mission, he should be diverted from
"his purpose by presents, and particularly of
"the herb of Paraguay. But if it should not
"be possible to dissuade him from his errand,
"by such an application to his interest, any
"and every means must be employed to frus-
"trate the object of it. 2d. If the commis-
"sary of finances, or any person employed by
"the king, should come into the country to
"impose taxes upon it, one half of the people
"must be sent into the mountains or forests,
"that he may not know the real population
"of the village. 3d. If the governor of Bue-
"nos Ayres, or any general or commanding
"officer should come to visit the villages of the
"mission, he should be loaded with presents,
"in order to turn him aside from his design:
"and if such means should not succeed, force
"itself must be employed to resist his preten-
"sions."

These instructions were sent into Europe, and exposed to imminent danger the life of the captain, whom the intrigues of the Jesuits retained in prison, at Ceuta, for two years, to prevent his appearing against them; they formed a principal instrument in the process which was instituted against the order in Spain.

Nevertheless, on an impartial examination of the preceding circumstances, the conduct of the Jesuits will be considered as not wholly unjustifiable, since their interests in these concerns was connected with that of a free people, who were oppressed on their account.* The Spaniards and Portuguese still enjoy the melancholy advantage derived from their con-

---

* It is not perhaps unnecessary to remark, that in France at that time, all the writers, except Dumouriez and some others, who were of Montesquieu's opinion, all inveighed bitterly against the republic of Paraguay. They had Voltaire at their head, and left no argument untried that could prove the bad tendency of that republic, and the justice, the utility, the necessity of exterminating its founders. The humane philosophers who are now preaching the freedom as well as the political liberty of the African slaves, could not suffer that civilization, equality, and a government purely evangelical, should be introduced among the free Americans of Paraguay; they preferred the military regulations of the Portuguese or Spanish commanders. How can such a contradiction be explained? Very easily. The Jesuits, whatever their politics might be, defended successfully by their writings against those philosophers, the Christian religion, which their missions propagated; and the state founded by them was a Christian commonwealth. The

quest of the Paraguay missions, which consists in nothing more than the dominion of a vast depopulated country.

To complete this state of mortification, the Jesuits, dispirited in America, and humiliated at Lisbon and Madrid, suffered in silence. In both these courts they conducted themselves with moderation and prudence, supporting their disgrace with apparent resignation, boldly disavowing all that had passed in Paraguay; declaring their submission, and brooding over their vengeance.

The assassination of the King of Portugal by penitents of the Jesuits, following hard upon the business of Paraguay, they were suspected of having resolved, by this crime, to revenge the injustice which they had suffered in America. The Fathers Malagrida, Matos, and Alexander, were arrested, put to the torture, and involved in the catastrophe of this conspiracy. All the possessions of the Jesuits were confiscated, and their resistance in Para-

---

black slaves, on the contrary, have no religion but their *Fetishism*, which is the worship of any living or inanimate being *ad libitum*: this must and will agree, better than any religious system whatever, with modern philosophism, and indefinite liberty. Ergo, &c. T.

guay seemed to justify the confiscation. At length they were all banished; and, in defiance of the Pope, the ecclesiastical states were over-run by 4000 persons, who being dismissed from their stations, were become altogether useless. The Nuntio, by the haughty manner in which he attempted to protect the power of the papal militia, rendered their situation still worse; while to hopeless banishment, and general confiscation, was added the sale of all their property.

The Nuntio however, extremely irritated, quitted Portugal; and the court of Rome, considering the process instituted against the Jesuits to be a wicked attempt, put the kingdom under an interdict. The minister being thus driven to an extremity, attacked the holy see itself. This first act of hostility was a book prepared under his inspection, (and as some have supposed, written by himself), to prove that the Popes ought not to have approved the institution of the Jesuits; and when they had done it, that they ought to have retracted their approbation, which might have been done without exposing their authority, because they are not infallible; and that even in the councils, there are examples of a similar recantation. This book having made the danger of a rigorous conduct evident to the court of Rome, it endeavoured to employ mediators to terminate the dispute in a friendly manner. But the minister was inflexible, and so far from seeking the favour of the holy see, he made another and still more forcible attack upon it last year, in bringing forward the Father Perreira, a celebrated theologian, to support a thesis, whose object was to prove the non-infallibility of the Pope. This thesis, sustained by the authority of the synods of France, and the canonical books of the French clergy, is full of strong argument, and written in a style of great animation. The effect of these hostilities against the court of Rome exasperated both parties; and it might have happened that the court of Portugal, after having adopted the liberty of the Gallican church, would not have stopped there; if the Patriarch of Lisbon had been a man of talents, and the Count d'Oeyras ten years younger.

CHAPTER IV.

UNIVERSITY OF COIMBRA, COLLEGE OF NOBLES; LITERATURE, AUTHORS, HISTORIANS, POETS, ARTS.

LITERATURE and the arts, and the means to make a progress in them, are extremely circumscribed in Portugal. The University of Coimbra, the parent of learning in this kingdom, is six centuries behind the enlightened parts of Europe. Nothing is known there but the Aristotelian philosophy, and the theological subtleties, so disgraceful to religion and the human understanding, which prevailed in that school in the earlier periods of the Christian era. This university contains 4000 scholars, who pass their lives in dissipation and ignorance. Their principal occupation is to make small tooth-picks of boxwood, known under the name of *palitos*. The class for the Greek tongue, in 1766, consisted of seven scholars.

The Jesuits were entrusted in Portugal, as in all the other catholic countries, with the education of youth. The Count d'Oeyras has filled up their place with a college of nobles, directed by himself, and opened in 1766. He chose very able professors on every branch of education; but the universality of its objects was blended with pedantry. To support this institution, he assigned the revenues of the Jesuits, or at least a principal part of them.

Literature is at a very low ebb in Portugal, though the Portuguese themselves neither want understanding or a disposition to cultivate it; but they have long been without any inducements to apply to learning; and it is but lately, that the young nobility have turned their attention to literary pursuits. They are passionately fond of Voltaire, Rousseau, and the new philosophy: and almost all the works of those authors are translated into the Portuguese language. The most distinguished among the young Fidalgos, by their application to learning, are the two Counts of Castlemelhor, the two Counts of Lavradio, the Marquis of Cascaes, the Counts de Prado, da Ponté, and one named Pinto; they form a small literary society in great estimation, and which has already given to the public a translation of the Theatre of Voltaire, of the Henriade, the Emilius, the Spirit of Laws, and the Art of War by the King of Prussia. Foreign authors on surgery and medicine, are continually translating, so that by degrees a taste will be formed in this country, and the Portuguese will quit their state of ignorance much sooner than the Spaniards. They are better furnished than them with ancient authors; their historians are excellent, though too much loaded with miracles and exaggerated relation. The first of them is John de Barros, the Livy of Portugal, who has written with great purity the Decades of the Indies. The editions of this book are very old and very scarce. The continuation by Diego Couto, does not equal it in force or elegance, in facility of narration, or in the grand style of its harangues; but the particulars in both authors are always interesting; and prolixity alone lessens the pleasure of reading their work. Manoel Faria, has written an history of Portugal, well written in the Spanish language. He lived in the time of the three Philips. The style of this author is good, and his turn satirical, nor is he less a lover of the marvellous than Barros. Jacinto Freira de Andrada, has written a life of Don Juan de Castro, in a style as bombastic as his hero is extravagant. This author has talent, and force of expression, but is always searching after quibbles and hyperbole. There are also some good chronicles. That of Resende, a Latin writer, takes the lead for antiquities, Damianus de Goes, for the reign of Don Manoel; Francisco de Andrada, for King John III. Buarte Nunhes de Leon, for John I. Edward, and Alphonso V. This author has also written the life of the ten first kings of Portugal, and the description of the kingdom. The re-conquest of Portugal by the Count de Ericeira, is highly spoken of, and translated into French. This writer loses himself in details, expresses his thoughts in a confused manner, and dwells upon trifles. This work contains an history of the war, from the revolution of 1640, to the peace in 1668. There are two indifferent treatises on fortification by Don Luis Serraon Pimentel, and Manoel Azevedo; a judicious treatise on navigation by Don Manoel Pimentel; and a new description of Portugal, by Caetano de Lima, which, though full of faults, is more correct than any other.

There is a considerable number of Portuguese poets, some of which have merit. But the first of them, and the most known in foreign countries, is Luis de Camoens. His poem, which is entitled the Lusiad, possesses a strong but easy versification. Its subject is the conquest of the Indies by Vasco de Gama, and is a servile imitation of the Odyssea, of the Eneid, and all the ancient poems. In one of its cantos, the author has introduced a noble and affecting episode of the death of Ines de Castro, mistress of King Don Pedro the just; On which subject Monsieur de la Motte has written a very fine tragedy; Ferreira, a Portuguese tragic author, has treated it with success, according to the rules of the Greek theatre, with choruses, &c. There also remains of this poet, an excellent translation of the Amphytrion, two other comedies, detached pieces of poetry, and a collection of charming letters written with great spirit and vivacity. There are many other poems in the Portuguese language, of which the least bad is Malaca Conquistado, or the conquest of Malacca.

At the close of the last century, and the beginning of the present, a celebrated preacher named Father Vieira, had been twice sent to the inquisition for having expressed himself with too much freedom in the pulpit, and also on an accusation of Judaism. The Pope was obliged to interpose, that he might not become a victim of that tribunal. He is the Bourdaloue* of this country.

Another Vieira is the best painter of Portugal, which has produced very few of any merit. The Portuguese physicians are very ignorant; while the surgeons are clumsy operators and great quacks. Lisbon has now a great musical composer, named David Perés, who is well known throughout Europe. But in this city there are teachers of dancing, fencing or horsemanship; though the Portuguese boast of admirable horsemen. Hence it is, that they are very deficient in all corporal exercises. It is, however, more than fifty years since the Portuguese were excellent swordmen; but, instead of using the points of their swords, they struck with the blade, which they named Pancada.

---

* A Jesuit, famous for the eloquence of his sermons, and the severity of his doctrine; the French call him the Demosthenes of the pulpit. His sermon on impureness, has been put in parallel with the discourse of the Greek orator, *pro Corona*. T.

CHAPTER V.

THE GOVERNMENT, THE MARINE, COMMERCE, AGRICULTURE, AND FINANCE.

All the different parts of society, like those of the body, depend upon each other, and the disease of the one necessarily influences the condition of all the rest. A superstitious people, who cultivate but in a small degree the arts and sciences, cannot possess a well regulated government. Besides, the subjection of the Portuguese to the English, diminishes the vigour which the Count d'Oeyras has laboured for the last fifteen years to communicate to all the relaxed springs of this machine. During the present century, the Portuguese government has been without strength, and without attention. The ministers slumbering at the foot of the throne, have suffered it to be shaken by the insolence of the nobles, the usurpations of ecclesiastics, and the tyranny of the English. Nature appears also to have assisted all these political causes of decay, in order to complete the ruin of Portugal, by an earthquake; and it is in the midst of these ruins, that the celebrated Sebastian Joseph Carvalho, Count d'Oeyras had the courage to re-establish the throne, by supporting it with one hand, whilst with the other he crushed the nobility, humbled the clergy, and diminished the influence of the English. The first enterprise of this great man excited fanatacism and conspiracies, and gave him an opportunity to display his severe and inflexible character. The king, escaped from the strokes of his assassins, became their master and their judge. After he had removed this first obstacle, the Minister attacked the ecclesiastics, and at length employed the most subtle policy respecting the English. Powerfully impelled by the same hatred of that nation as the Portuguese universally possess, he directed his strokes against them, under the semblance of measures for rectifying abuses.

The marine was in a very bad state. Five or six disabled ships and as many frigates, without sailors or officers, constituted the whole naval force of Portugal. The Minister, in order to become absolute master of this department, obtained the post of secretary of the marine for his brother Francis Xavier de Mendoça, who died about three years ago. He was a man of a narrow capacity, but very industrious, and perfectly submissive to his brother. Accordingly, in about seven or eight years the marine was established upon a good footing; at the same time, the English, the Swedes, the Dutch, the Danes, and the French were invited to teach navigation to the Portuguese; who, two centuries ago, conquered three quarters of the globe, carried on the commerce of it, and directed all its views to the improvement of its marine. The actual state of its navy consists of ten ships of the line, and double that number of frigates, all built of the finest Brasil timber. Two ships have been launched at Lisbon of 74 and 72 guns, and admirably constructed for resistance as well as duration. But neither the officers or the sailors are kept in sufficient practice; and I am of opinion, that vessel against vessel, the Spaniards would beat them at sea, from the superiority of their equipage. But this deficiency may always be supplied by the English navy. The present state, however, of the Portuguese marine, is sufficient to protect the coasts, and the war against the Algerines, and the corsairs of Salé, may serve as a school to teach the art of naval combat, and accustom them to it, which is the more necessary as they have not the reputation of being brave at sea. The war with Morocco may be, one day or other, fatal to the Portuguese: for if the Emperor should fortify Mogadore, invite to his service renegade seamen, and order his corsairs to cruize about the Cape Verde Islands, the Canaries, Açores, and Madeira, the ships coming from Brasil would risk being often taken.

The commerce of Portugal, notwithstanding all the efforts of the Count d'Oeyras, is altogether in the hands of the English, to whom the Portuguese are no more than brokers or agents, and even English ships are employed in the whole of their trade, except that of the Indies, of Africa, and America; which is under the direction of distinct companies, and carried on by the king's ships; but even in those branches of commerce the Portuguese, though they lend their names, are not principals. The most considerable factories of Brasil and Africa belong to English capitalists, who have for correspondents the English houses of Lisbon, Oporto, and London, of whom the Portuguese themselves purchase the merchandize that comes from their own colonies.

The Count d'Oeyras, after a very attentive consideration of this subject, determined upon a very singular operation, which was no less than to change the general order of commerce. He accordingly abolished all the old trading companies, and destroyed their exclusive rights; while, on the contrary, he erected new companies, and gave them an exclusive right over those branches of commerce which had hitherto been free. But notwithstanding all his care and precautions, the English, from their large capitals, became the masters in these new arrangements, and, under borrowed names, possessed themselves of all the new funds. Another evil has arisen from this new arrangement, which the Minister did not foresee, but which caused the seditious discontents that have prevailed in Brasil, and threatened the total ruin of the colonies. The companies having obtained permission from different ministers, and particularly from Count d'Oeyras, to impose duties both on the sale of their own merchandize, and the purchase of the produce of the country, these duties proved very burdensome to the inhabitants of Brasil; they became, on account of them, very much indebted to these companies, who, on their abolition, demanded payment. Accordingly the Count d'Oeyras found himself obliged to take those measures which have dissatisfied both parties. Nevertheless, the merchants who continued the trade after the abolition of the companies, determined to carry on their sales, and make their purchases on the same principle as the companies had done; this produced a state of disorder and confusion in Brasil, for which it was not easy to find a remedy.

The Count d'Oeyras aimed another blow at the interests of England, by encouraging a trade with France for grain; and in the year 1766, that country had made very profitable returns from Portugal, under the wise and able administration of the Duke de Choiseul. In this particular the Count d'Oeyras has found the means to diminish in Lisbon the general dependance on the English merchants. But this branch of commerce, after all, must be precarious and temporary, at least till the marine of France becomes strong enough to form a balance to that of Great Britain.

This successful essay has given birth to another attempt, which has been equally fortunate: to weaken the credit of the English respecting grain, and to lessen their immense profits on the wines of Portugal, the Minister ordered a considerable part of the vineyards to be destroyed, and sown with grain. This unreserved proceeding at once discovered his design, and produced a great clamour against him. The individuals also, whom he was determined to force into a new and more difficult cultivation of their ground, exclaimed against his tyranny, and refused to obey: but he was deaf to their clamours, rigorously insisted upon obedience, and forced his edict to be observed.

In order to understand this extraordinary operation, it is necessary to be informed, that Portugal is all vineyard, except some small cantons in Entre Minho e Douro, and Traz os Montes. The English have purchased, and consequently possess all the prime land in the environs of Oporto, and Lisbon, of Setuval, and Faro, whose wines are the best, and some of them in great estimation; so that the soil of Portugal and its productions may be said to belong to them. These circumstances, which are ruinous to the Portuguese, serve to prove their indolent disposition; of which they do not perceive the disadvantage. They prefer the culture of the vine, which requires but little trouble, to a more laborious cultivation.

The commerce of Portugal being entirely in the hands of the English, and being destitute of pasturage and grain, this kingdom is in an absolute state of dependance, because England furnishes it with all the commodities of which it stands in need. Such are the bonds of servitude that keep Portugal in that alliance with England, which the Count d'Oeyras has endeavoured to destroy. He also attacked the English interest, by establishing manufactures for silk, woollen-drapery, leather, and soap. At the same time he published very severe edicts to prohibit the importation of foreign stuffs: but the imperfect fabric of these manufactures, their slow progress, their bad quality, and high price, established the preference given to the silks, the woollens, and leather of England and France, and in spite of the edicts, the importation of foreign manufactures still prevails.

This Minister employed all his power to invite by treaties the commerce of Denmark, of Sweden, and of Russia, to Lisbon. This was a wise and beneficial measure, because the greater the number of foreigners concerned in the trade of Portugal, the less would remain in possession of England. But it was doing things only by halves, to establish a merely passive commerce. The Portuguese themselves should have been encouraged to navigate the distant seas, and to fetch foreign commodities in their own vessels; in short, to engage in an active commerce.

The Count d'Oeyras has agriculture very much at heart, regarding it as the basis of all government. He resolved to make a general register of the lands in order to ascertain their value, and to discover the means to be employed for bringing them into a state of cultivation; but after all the pains and time employed on this subject, and the calculations made, the lands in question remain untouched by the plough. The whole province of Alemtejo is uncultivated: Beira and Algarve continue to be a desert.

The finances of Portugal have been the first objects of attention to the Count d'Oeyras; and he reserved this department to himself, though without attaching any title to it. But the opinions on the state of the finances, and the revenues of the kingdom are various. It is indeed generally said that the treasury is full, that Portugal is very rich, and that its revenues are considerable; but there is great reason surely to suspect that the finances cannot be in a very good condition in a kingdom which has neither agriculture nor a marine; which has lately sustained an earthquake that produced so many large bankruptcies, and has been engaged in a very expensive war; whose colonies, which are a principal source of its riches, are so poor, so ill administered, and so harassed, that the people either leave them or revolt;. above all, if it is considered that this kingdom has many old debts, and that its wealth, particularly its gold, passes through the hands of the English, who derive all the advantage from it; and lastly, that the diamonds, of which it possesses a very large store, are a kind of dead stock, which does not enter into circulation. The Portuguese have but very few taxes to pay; nevertheless they live in a state of extreme wretchedness.

Previous to the ministry of the Count d'Oeyras, the finances of Portugal were in a most deplorable state of administration, 22,000 clerks or writers, divided into a considerable number of offices, devoured the revenues, embroiled the accounts, and swallowed up the treasure. The Minister, by a single edict of the month of October 1761, reduced this enormous crowd of blood-suckers to *thirty-two* well qualified and chosen persons. He has simplified the regulations relative to the receipts and payments of the public treasure, by using the same journals as bankers and merchants employ for the insertion of their daily transactions. These books are examined every week; while the king passes the accounts which are presented to him, or gives instructions concerning such as are in a state of preparation; none of which, however, are suffered to be in arrear. The perspicuity, the precision, and the security of this arrangement will appear incomprehensible in the different countries of Europe, where finance is so complicated a science, and such an inextricable labyrinth; but to convince incredulity, it is necessary only to have recourse to Portugal, and to read the edict of the Count d'Oeyras, and the execution of this plan will be instantly verified.

Here are many varying opinions respecting the revenues of Portugal, which some have calculated at seventy, and others at eighty millions of livres, or between three and four millions sterling. The mines produce annually from fifty to sixty millions of livres, or between two and three millions sterling.

CHAPTER VI.

THE COURT.

The court of Portugal is very dull and ceremonious. The king never sees the foreign ministers but on public days, and the rest of his time he passes with his family, or in hunting, of which he is passionately fond. This prince neither sees or does any thing but through his Minister, in whom he has placed the most unlimited confidence. He is peculiarly robust and indefatigable; is very grave, and seldom accessible at Lisbon. He passes two months, towards Lent, at Salvaterra, upon the left bank of the Tagus, where he is the most magnificent sovereign in Europe. He there entertains, at his own expence, all foreigners who are properly introduced. He maintains an excellent opera, and furnishes every one with horses for the chase. He passes some time also at Pinheiro, upon the banks of the Caldao, and at the Abbey of Mafra. But at these latter places travellers do not find any accommodation whatever.

The queen of Portugal preserves a rooted aversion to the court of France, where she had been sent in order to share the throne of Louis XV. She has not yet lost the remembrance of her forced return to the court of Spain. She is much attached to the king, whom she accompanies every where. She loves hunting as well as his majesty; and her continual equestrian exercises have tanned her face, and given it a ruddy and swarthy hue. She is very well informed, and not only possesses wit, but discretion. It was by her negotiations that the danger of the Spanish arms was averted in 1762. She detests the Count d'Oeyras, who troubles himself very little about her; but she does not venture to declare her sentiments respecting him. All her favourites have fallen a prey to the hatred of this Minister, who involved them in the executions which followed the conspiracy against the person of the king. Among others the Count d'Obidos, one of the most powerful nobles of Portugal, who had nothing to do with the conspiracy lost his liberty by a *bon mot*. There is a popular tradition relative to the King Don Sebastian, which the Portuguese believe. They say that he is not dead, but will return by sea to Lisbon, and resume the crown. One day, as the queen was at a window with her court, a large waterspout appeared on the sea, when the queen humorously observed, that it was King Don Sebastian returning; no, answered the Count d'Obidos, that is impossible, Don Sebastian is already here; it is he who reigns. Within two hours after this pleasantry, the Count was arrested and thrown into a dungeon in the castle of St. Julian, for the rest of the life of Count d'Oeyras, whose name is Sebastian Carvalho. This event brings to my recollection a lively observation of Lord Tyrawley: " What can be done with a nation, one half " of which expects a Messiah; and the other, " the King Don Sebastian, who has been dead " these 200 years?"

The queen has two daughters, the oldest of which is married to the Infant Don Pedro, a devout, gloomy, and silent character, by whom she has had the Prince de Beira, who is the presumptive heir of the crown. The second daughter is a very fine woman, well educated, and highly accomplished. This young princess had been proposed as a wife to the king of the Romans; but the then existing politics and the circumstances of the war prevented the execution of that design.

The old Prince Emanuel, the king's uncle, who died this year, had been a gallant prince, and had run through Europe to gratify his love of pleasure. There are no persons of high distinction at this court, but the young Duke of Cadaval, a man of a confined understanding, and a drunkard; and the Marquis of Marialva, a man of wit, an ancient chevalier, and uncommonly dexterous in all bodily exercises, as well as his two sons. The father of the Duke of Cadaval, a prince of the blood, was very much esteemed in the time of John V. for his wit, his satirical turn, his resolution, and his merit, I have seen at the Fathers of the Oratory; a large folio, entitled, *Ultimas Palavras do celebre Duque de Cadaval*: the last words of the Duke of Cadaval. The king has several illegitimate brothers; one of which is the archbishop of Braga; the others were thrown into prison at the epocha of the assassination. Don Joaõ de Bragança,* a prince of the blood, has

* This prince, called Duke da Lafoens, came at that time to England, where he remained about a year. T.

found security in a foreign residence. He became a lieutenant-general in the Austrian service, where he distinguished himself by his valour and his talents.

The two persons the best known in the ministerial party, and who may succeed to Count d'Oeyras, are Don Martin de Mello, and Don Joseph de Sylva Passanha. The first is ambassador in England, a man of talents, and attached to the English. The other, who is a wise and well informed person, and animated with the common hatred of England, is without employment, after having long been ambassador at the courts of Naples and Madrid. The rest of the nobility never approach the king: without credit, money, power, or honours, they cringe before the Count d'Oeyras and his wife, while the princes of the blood, the nobles, and the people, all unite in caressing and detesting that powerful family.

CHAPTER VII.

A SUMMARY OF THE HISTORY OF PORTUGAL.

The kingdom of Portugal is known in ancient history by the name of Lusitania. Its people maintained themselves against the inroads of the Romans, whom they have often conquered, under the command of Viriatus,* who being the captain of a banditti, became the general of an army, and made the Romans tremble; and

---

* In the reign of King John III. upon removing some ruins on the land of a Pedro Machado Corregueiro, in the territory of Belas, near Lisbon, they found accidentally the tomb of Viriatus; it was a stone chest with this inscription upon it, *Hic jacet Viriatus Lusitanus Dux.* Within there was a sword, on which were engraved many characters. Pedro Machado desiring to sell this piece of antiquity, (whether of the Roman age or posterior to it) offered it successively to all the great men in the kingdom; but none of them choosing to buy it, he at last gave Viriatus's tomb to a friend, who lived in the island of Madeira, where it was carried and lost. T.

Sertorius, a Roman commander, whose discontents made him the enemy of his country. The Romans were not able to overcome the Lusitanians, till they had procured the assassination of these two generals.

When the Roman empire became a prey to the barbarians, the Alani got possession of the country situated between the Minho and the Tagus, where they founded a kingdom; which after having been conquered by the Goths, became with them a prey to the Arabians: the capital of this kingdom was Coimbra. Alphonso VI. King of Leon and Castile, having commenced with advantage the war against the Moors, engaged a considerable number of knights from France, Gascony, Italy, and England, to fight with him in a war against the Infidels. The most distinguished of these knights was Henry of the house of Burgundy. The king, to fix him in his country, gave him his illegitimate daughter Theresa in marriage, and Galicia for her dowry, with whatever he could conquer of Portugal, and the title of Count. This prince accordingly carried on the war with so much vigour, that he conquered all the country to the banks of the Tagus. His son, Alphonso Henriquez, having overcome five kings, or rather five Moorish governors, caused himself to be declared king in the year 1135. He pretended that Jesus Christ had commanded him to do it; that his crucifix had extended its arms and spoken to him. Twenty-five kings, since that epocha, have governed Portugal. I must refer to the history of the kingdom at large, all those who wish to inform themselves of the particulars of their respective reigns, and confine myself to some slight sketches of their more striking events.

At the commencement of the fourteenth century, the King Denis drove the Moors entirely out of Algarve, by taking Faro, which was their last retreat. He also added to Portugal the little country called Riba de Coa, that is washed by the Coa, a small river, on whose banks is situated Almeida, which is the capital. This King Denis suffered great uneasiness from the conduct of his son, who afterwards succeeded him under the name of Alphonso IV. and who was surnamed the African, from having made the conquest of Tangier, Ceuta, Safia, Tetuan, and Mazagan.

The son of Alphonso IV. was Don Pedro I. celebrated by the death of his wife, the unfortunate Ines de Castro, and by the cruelties that accompanied his vengeance. One of the assassins was named *Coelho*, which in the Portuguese language signifies a rabbit. Don Pedro therefore ordered him to be spitted, roasted, and served up to his accomplices. Portugal has had the rare fortune of having a much greater number of good than bad kings. John I. whom victory and the love of the people raised to the throne, although illegitimate; and Alphonso and John III. distinguished by the title of the perfect prince, were great kings, and made Portugal flourish.

But the most brilliant epocha of this kingdom, was that of the Kings Don Emanuel and John III. The first of these princes had an uncle named Cardinal Don Henry, who resided at Lagos in Algarve. This prince who was rich, engaged, by large rewards, two gentlemen, named Tristan Vaz, and Zarco, to attempt discoveries on the western part of Africa; and it is to the encouragement which he gave to navigation, that the Portuguese owe their conquests. Soon after, Alvaro Cabral, and Vasco de Gama, made separate discoveries of Brasil and the Indies. At the end of fifty years, the Portuguese found themselves, by their courage, masters of all the coast of Africa, from Cape Blanco to the island of Socotora, and from Cape Guadarfui, the whole compass of Asia, the Red Sea, the Gulf of Ormuz, the two Peninsulas of the Ganges, and the Molucca Islands were in their hands. They possessed the entire trade in gold, silks, porcelain, pearls, and ivory; in short all the commodities of three parts of the globe, which were known only to them. But it was not long before the European powers became jealous of their greatness.

A terrible and unexpected revolution changed in one moment the face of Portugal: the most fatal of all events precipitated the Portuguese from the height of their glory, and reduced them to the greatest misery. Don Sebastian, a young prince of the greatest hopes, at once courageous and indefatigable, possessed of the most active and solid talents, ascended the throne in 1572, with a determination to render himself illustrious by some splendid action. Inspired by the ardour of chivalry, he meditated nothing less than the conquest of Africa and its infidel inhabitants. He assembled an army of 20,000 men, composed of his principal nobility, and the flower of his subjects. He placed himself at their head, and passed into Africa, where he was conquered and slain at the battle of Alcazarquivir,* with the greatest part of the Portuguese nobility. The Portuguese, a credulous people, and who love the marvellous, then pretended, and still believe, as has been already mentioned, that he is not dead. Philip II. King of Spain, the Duke of Bragança, and an illegitimate uncle of Don Sebastian, were competitors for the crown; which, after the death or disappearance of Don Sebastian, was possessed by an old cardinal, named Don Henry, who reigned but a few months. Philip maintained his rights with an experienced army, conducted by the celebrated Duke of Alba. In vain did the Portuguese, excited rather by their hatred of the Castilians, than any attachment to the bastard Don Antonio, made some feeble efforts to avoid the Spanish yoke. The disaster of Don Sebastian had left them without troops,

* Or al Caszr in the kingdom of Fez. Don Sebastian went to assist Muley Mahomed, king of Morocco, against Muley Mulack, his uncle and king of Fez, by whom he had been dethroned. They fought in 1578, and the three kings perished in the battle. An adventurer appeared in Portugal in 1601, who pretended to be Don Sebastian, and had many followers. T.

without a fleet, and without money. None of the powers of Europe supported their cause, and in two months they were entirely subjugated.

The epocha of Don Sebastian cast a funereal veil over the Portuguese nation. All the ancient families were interrupted in their successions by the havock of war; all the national force was exhausted by the loss of the army; all conquests were at an end: and during the reigns of the three Castilian kings, named the three Philips, nothing is seen in this unfortunate kingdom but disgrace, rebellion, and disasters. This catastrophe was in 1580, and the captivity of Portugal, or its submission to Spain, lasted sixty years. The Dutch availed themselves of the weakness of Portugal, and of the little assistance afforded it by Spain, which was itself in a languishing condition during the reigns of the three Philips, and formed establishments at Olinda, and Fernambucco in Brasil. They possessed these colonies during thirty years, drove the Portuguese from the Molucca Islands, those of the isles of Sunda, Ceylon, &c. and acquired the sovereignty of the Indian seas, which the Portuguese had possessed during the glorious reigns of Don Emanuel, and John III. They established the important settlement of the Cape of Good Hope, and during these sixty years, they despoiled Portugal of all its power. It was by those seizures of the Portuguese possessions, that the Dutch avenged themselves of the Spanish nation.

Misfortune now seemed to have attained its height. Portugal, at once harassed and despised, appeared to be too feeble to be an object of the least consideration. The court of Madrid punished the complaints of despair, and fancied that despair was impotent; when the patience of the Portuguese was, at length, exhausted. In 1640, thirty gentlemen, without communicating their project, and without being assured of any support, murdered Vasconcelos, who tyrannized over the people, under a princess of Austria, appointed to govern the kingdom, for Philip IV. The fire of rebellion spread around, and soon became universal; and in so small a space as a month, all the Spaniards were driven away, and with little effusion of blood. The timid Duke of Bragança was forced by his wife to mount a dubious throne, under the name of John IV. This irresolute prince was by no means worthy of ruling a brave people, but the nation was determined to support him; and continued to maintain a war against Spain during twenty-eight years, with great courage and equal success. Neither the death of this king, nor that of prince Theodosius who succeeded him, and whom the nation regarded as a rising hero, nor the reign of that weak monarch Alphonso VI. could diminish the enthusiasm of the Portuguese, nor restore to the Spaniards their former superiority. After having lost four battles in Portugal, the Spaniards gave up the design of re-entering that kingdom. The same spirit of liberty communicated itself to the Portuguese colonies; the Spaniards were driven from Goa, and all the Portuguese settlements in India; from Congo, and the presidencies of Africa, and Brasil.

At length, in 1668, King Charles II. was forced to grant peace to the King Don Pedro II. the brother and successor of King Alphonso VI. and to acknowledge him as king of Portugal; at the same time renouncing all pretensions to that crown. Alphonso VI. possessed a very weak understanding, and a very violent temper; he had married a princess of the blood of France, named Louisa d'Orleans, who, instigated by the Count Schomberg, and shocked at the insolence of Count Castelmelhor, the favourite of Alphonso and absolute master of the kingdom, had the boldness to accuse her husband of impotency and madness, and to sue for a separation before the states of the kingdom. Don Pedro, the brother of the king, was entrusted with the care of the kingdom and of Queen Louisa, who was become pregnant. Alphonso in a second assembly of the states, was declared unworthy of his kingdom, and unfit to have a wife; accordingly he was deprived of both, and they were given to Don Pedro. Alphonso was shut up, and suffered enough to make him mad, if he was not so before. The Pope was bribed with considerable sums to pardon all these acts of injustice, and a splendid *auto da fé* appeased the anger of God.

Don Pedro peaceably enjoyed his good fortune, and transmitted his kingdom to his son John V. Portugal, since the peace of 1668, has resumed its ancient constitution, but it has not been able to attain its former vigour. Its powerful protectors, and the change it has undergone, leave it but a secondary place in the scale of Europe: it was now become subordinate to England, whose forced alliance is a strong indissoluble chain, and its weight daily is increasing.

CHAPTER VIII.

ANECDOTES——JOHN V., JOSEPH I.; THE EARTHQUAKE; THE CONSPIRACY; THE WAR OF 1762; THE LOSS OF THE CUSTOMHOUSE BY FIRE; THE DEATH OF GRAVERON; THE REVOLT OF BRASIL.

THE history of Portugal conducts us to the reign of John V. I shall therefore reduce to certain anecdotes all I have to say respecting that king, and the monarch now on the throne; and will pursue my plan without flattery and without passion. John V. who filled the throne of Portugal at the beginning of the present century, reigned with honour and happiness. He was a prince of superior understanding, great in all his designs, magnificent, gallant, and proud. He possessed all the qualities of Louis XIV. and resembled him in every thing but his love of war, which John abhorred. He was much attached to his alliance with England, and did not sufficiently reflect on the empire that greedy nation usurped over his country. He had conceived a violent friendship for Lord Tyrawley, the English ambassador, who availed himself of this partiality to become the most insolent of favourites, and to load with injury and contempt the Portuguese nation. This king made himself respected by his neighbours, both by his wisdom and his resolution; when, in the war which placed Don Carlos upon the throne of Naples, he was menaced by Spain. On that occasion, he raised in the course of three months, an army of 35,000 men, commanded by able officers, with a numerous artillery and a respectable marine. This vigorous conduct procured him a solid peace, which the flame of discord lighted up throughout Europe in 1741 did not interrupt. In the bosom of peace he sought for solid glory. He greatly embellished the royal palace, of which not a single vestige remains. He built a magnificent patriarchal church, which became also a prey to the earthquake. He erected the sumptuous convent of Mafra, at four leagues distance from Lisbon, where he formed a very valuable library. He also caused an aqueduct to be erected to conduct water to Lisbon; a work worthy the genius of the ancient Romans, and which even the earthquake seems to have respected. In short, he made his subjects happy, and was adored by them. But this prince having fallen, at the close of his life, into a state of extreme devotion, abandoned the care of public affairs to Gaspard, his confessor, the relation and protector of young Carvalho. He dissipated the greatest part of his revenues in establishing chapels, building convents, and paying for masses. It became at last a matter of obligation to prevent his becoming acquainted with the deaths that happened at Lisbon; as he no sooner knew of the death of any of his subjects, though among the very lowest classes, but he ordered an hundred masses or more to be said at his expence. His devotion became more and more extravagant, till it degenerated into absolute imbecillity, and he died almost an idiot.

The reign of Joseph I. was destined to experience the greatest dangers, and the most uncommon catastrophes. This king having ascended the throne in 1750, found his treasury empty, his government oppressed with debts, and the English masters of the kingdom and its colonies. His minister, Diego de Mendoça, had not sufficient talents to apply a remedy to these abuses. Carvalho, returned from the embassy of Vienna, obtained the confidence of the king, turned out the minister, who was banished to Mazagan, and took his place. He passed the two or three first years of his ministry in contending with cabals, in searching into the causes of the deranged state of government, and in suffering the insolence of the nobles, who wished to pull him down.

On the first of November, 1755, happened the famous earthquake which desolated all Portugal, threw down a considerable number of buildings in every town throughout the kingdom, and destroyed, as it were, in the same hour, 50,000 people. But Lisbon suffered most; the earthquake there assumed its most terrific form. The elements united to overwhelm the wretched inhabitants; the sea and the river rushed into the city, the earth opened wide its jaws, and fire consumed their dwellings. It was the festival of All-saints, and at nine in the morning, when great numbers of people were hearing mass. The churches were thrown down, and all those whom devotion or alarm had conducted thither, were crushed beneath their fall. The aged, the infants, and the sick, were smothered in their beds, or consumed by the flames, which were blown into fury by the tempest that accompanied the earthquake. The vessels in the harbour were violently driven against each other, and many of them perished. But in the midst of this general desolation, an horrid scene of human brutality was displayed, and added to the universal horror of the moment. The desire of plunder, inflamed with the hope of speedy success a large band of sailors, soldiers, negroes, and criminals, whom this event had delivered from their prisons: these infamous wretches spread themselves throughout the city, to increase by pillage, violation, and murder, the horrors that surrounded them. To complete the calamity, Lisbon was threatened with famine; while the stench of the dead bodies corrupted the air, and produced symptoms of plague.

The Count d'Oeyras alone preserved a presence of mind in this scene of desolation; and where the fear of the future stifled all complaints at the present evil. This Minister took no repose; and having no other dwelling, or bed, or office, but his coach, was seen every where, encouraging and consoling the wretched inhabitants. In eight days he published 230 ordinances to regulate the circumstances of the moment; which have been collected in one large volume, entitled, *Providencias sobre os terremotos*. He caused the fire to be extinguished, he ordered all the dead bodies to be covered with quick lime, or thrown into the sea; he directed the public ways to be opened through the ruins; he encouraged the garrison; and condemned the banditti, who infested the city, to suffer military execution. Provisions of all kinds were fetched from the provinces, by land and by sea; and by his example and resolution, he stopped the people who were determined to abandon a country which had so often been laid waste by similar destruction. But notwithstanding all the care and precautions of Count d'Oeyras, who was at this time the tutelary deity and saviour of Lisbon, besides the loss of lives, of effects, and furniture, there was lost in merchandize, money, and bankruptcies, produced by this terrible event, above six millions sterling. Of the magnificent palace of the kings of Portugal, not one stone remained upon another. Immense riches were there devoured by the flames, as well as in the patriarchal church, or were buried in their ruins. The court, full of alarm and agitation during eight days, had no other asylum but such as they found in their carriages, and the garden of Bellem, a small villa about a league from Lisbon. The king and the royal family, while they displayed the utmost resignation for themselves, exercised all their charity in consoling the unhappy people; and offered to their view an affecting example of greatness of mind, and patient resolution.

The recompence of Carvalho for his magnanimous conduct on this fatal occasion, was the entire and irrevocable confidence of the king. This was no more than an act of justice to that able Minister, but it heightened to an extreme degree of rage the jealousy of his numerous enemies: strengthened, however, by the sovereign power, he began to take very strong measures: he attacked at once the departments of the marine, of commerce, and of the finances, as well as the clergy, the nobility, and the Jesuits: the latter were the first objects of his resentment, and the conquest of Paraguay was decided and arranged by the court of Madrid. The grandees irritated and alarmed, felt their own weakness; nor had they the courage to make a direct attack upon this superior character, whose very looks they were afraid to encounter. Vengeance is the element of the Portuguese, but they prefer those modes of indulging it which are not liable to danger; they do not, therefore, consider assassination as a crime, because, as Moliere says,* it is the surest way to get rid of an anemy.

An horrible conspiracy was plotting with the utmost secrecy; four persons in the state were concerned in it: the Duke d'Aveiro, of the house of Mascarenhas, who was the head of it, was allied to the royal family. Mordomo-mor grandmaster, or steward of the king's household, and the most powerful nobleman of Portugal; he was an ugly, little man, of a narrow mind, but vain and wrongheaded, deranged in his affairs, capable of any crimes, always cringing to the Minister, whom he detested, while he himself was universally hated and despised. This man was easily excited to commit any crime by the Marchioness de Tavora, who was the soul of the conspiracy. That lady, one of the finest women in Europe, of a superior genius and ambition, capable of every thing whether good or bad, was dreaded

* In his comedy of the *Sicilien* or *L'amour Peintre.* T.

at court on account of her violent disposition, haughty spirit, and sarcastic pleasantries; she was the declared enemy of Carvalho, and never spoke of him but in the most reproachful terms, nor did she treat the king with more respect, whose whole conduct was the public object of her satirical insults; equally the enemy of the queen and the princesses, she treated them as her equals. But this terrible woman had a great number of followers, powerful vassals, as well as large estates. Her magnificence, her profusion, her winning looks, gained the affections of the people, whom she managed with great address. She blended her criminal disposition and her pride with extreme devotion, and was under the direction of an old Jesuit, named Malagrida, a fanatical and visionary character, who believed himself to be inspired. Her husband, a general of cavalry, her two children, her son-in-law, the Count of Atouguia, and her daughter-in-law, the Marchioness of Tavora, were also under the spiritual direction of the Jesuits, and subject to the will of this imperious woman. It was said in Portugal that the conspirators had no design to hurt the king, and that their sole object was Carvalho. This opinion was founded upon the circumstance that it was in the carriage of the Minister the attempt was made upon the king; and as the royal coaches had passed on before without having been attacked, it has a claim to some degree of credit. After all, the profound mystery in which the whole proceeding was involved, allows little more than conjecture.

The conspiracy in the mean time was carried on with great secrecy and equal indiscretion. The Duke d'Aveiro, the Marquis de Tavora, his two sons, the Count d'Atouguia, the Almeidas, and the Sousas, were the respectable names which appeared at the head of 250 persons of both sexes, who were accomplices without the secret having transpired: nevertheless, the Duke d'Aveiro, proud at one moment, and cringing at another, rendered himself suspected by his menaces and indiscreet discourse. Love had also its share in this cruel scene. The young Marchioness de Tavora carried on an intrigue with the king, which all her family considered as an affront, and they availed themselves of the mysterious visit which he paid every day to this lady.

On the day appointed to carry this horrid plot into execution, 3d September, 1758, the conspirators, to the number of 150, divided themselves into small troops, and took post in different parts of the way which the king was to pass. His majesty was in a calash, drawn by two mules, conducted by one postilion, and was accompanied only by his valet de chambre. The first band of conspirators let him pass on till he was in the midst of them, when they discharged forty-muskets;* the calash was pierced in various places, and the king received three wounds, the most considerable of which was in his shoulder. His valet de chambre, whose name was Texeira, had the presence of mind to make the king truckle down at the bottom of the chaise, that he might sit over him, and at all risks cover his body. At the same time, the postillion, as brave and as faithful as Texeira, instead of pursuing the road, or returning back again, turned with great address, and with the utmost speed, into a bye way, amidst many other random shots, and by a circuitous road got back to the palace of

* Two men only fired at the king's calash, Ferreira, who was executed, and Azevedo, who by his early escape, shewed himself the only one among so many conspirators that foresaw what would happen afterwards. See the note next to this. T.

Bellem. These two men, to whom the king owed his life, were amply recompensed.

The king on arriving at the palace, covered himself with a cloak belonging to one of his guards, ordered Carvalho to be instantly called to him, and waited at the gate, without thinking of his wounds, or discovering the least sign of pain or apprehension. The Minister with his usual resolution, and maintaining the same magnanimity as his master, prohibited Texeira, the postillion, and guards, from making any discovery of what had happened. He also recommended to the king himself silence and dissimulation. Nevertheless, the news of this event having spread abroad, perhaps by the conspirators themselves, the people ran in a state of alarm and confusion to Bellem, and the nobles repaired to the palace. The Duke d'Aveiro appeared the most anxious and alarmed of them all, and offered to place himself at the head of the cavalry to go in search of the assassins. But Carvalho removed his fears, pretended to make him his confident, and with a mysterious air, recommended him to appear to know nothing of the matter: nevertheless, the Minister already suspected him, from the knowledge he had of his turbulent spirit, and the well known hatred he bore to himself. The king, to dissipate the fears of his people, appeared at a window, and declared from thence, that the report of his assassination was false, that the slight hurt he had received was from no other cause but the accidental overturning of his calash. To confirm this belief, he engaged in his usual exercises even before he was cured of his wounds, and the agitated spirit of the people was universally quieted: even the conspirators themselves, deceived by the general tranquillity, took no precautions whatever to prevent discovery, and remained at ease. One alone, named Polycarp, a domestic of the Tavora family, being suspicious of this mysterious state of inaction quitted the kingdom.

Nevertheless Carvalho, in secrecy and in silence, took his measures to discover the authors of the conspiracy, and chance discovered them to him. A valet had an intrigue with a servant of the household of Tavora, and used to meet her lover in the gardens. One night, while he was waiting for his mistress, the conspirators assembled near the spot where he was concealed; and after they had conversed about the plot that had failed, unfolded the design of another. The valet heard all, and gave immediate information to the Minister; who, on continuing his inquiries, found his suspicions confirmed, and was soon possessed of sufficient proofs of the conspiracy, and the persons concerned in it. The more Carvalho thought Aveiro and Tavora criminal, the more he flattered and caressed them. The first of them, through fear, and perhaps by the advice of his accomplices, who were more prudent than himself, asked permission to pass one month at his country seat, under the pretext of re-establishing his health. Carvalho immediately obtained leave for three months. The other had formerly solicited a commandry, and the Minister now announced a grant of it, on the part of the king. In short, his Majesty and the Minister so conducted themselves, that the people not only ceased to speak of the assassination, but even to remember any thing concerning it.

Nevertheless, in about six months, Carvalho proposed the marriage of his daughter with the Count of Sampayo, a nobleman of high birth. The king accordingly signed the contract of marriage, and took upon himself the expences of the wedding. All the grandees of the kingdom were invited to assist at the ceremony; and the Duke d'Aveiro returned in great haste to Lisbon to be present at it. Ten battalions and as many squadrons of troops arrived the same night, and at the same hour in the capital. There were two balls which occupied the attention of the city; the one at Bellem, given by the Minister, and the other at the Long Room, a place of entertainment belonging to foreign merchants, who gave it in honour of the marriage. At the same hour all the conspirators were arrested, their palaces invested, and the process against them being already prepared, ten of the principal of them were executed in the course of a week, in the square of the palace of Bellem. The Duke d'Aveiro was drawn into quarters by horses,* the Marquis de Tavora;

---

* The General is far from being correct in the particulars of this bloody scene, which is the more surprising as the following account was published by authority after the execution.

"Saturday, January 18, 1759, a scaffold having been
"built in the square opposite to the house where the
"prisoners were confined, eight wheels were fixed
"upon it: on one corner of the scaffolding was placed
"Antonio Alvares Ferreira, and at the other corner
"the effigy of Joseph Policarpio de Azevedo, who is
"still missing; these being the two persons who fired

his two sons, his wife, and the Count d'Atouguia his son-in-law, were beheaded, and four inferior accomplices were burned alive. Aveiro died like a coward. The rest supported their torments with resolution. But the two criminals who displayed the greatest strength of

"at the king's equipage. About half an hour after
" eight o'clock in the morning the execution began.
" The Marchioness Tavora was the first who was
" brought upon the scaffold, when she was beheaded
" at one stroke. Her body was afterwards placed upon
" the floor of the scaffolding, and covered with a linen
" cloth. Young Joseph Maria of Tavora, the young
" Marquis of Tavora, the Count of Atouguia, and three
" servants of the Duke of Aveiro, were first strangled
" at a stake, and afterwards their limbs broken with
" an iron instrument; the Marquis of Tavora, gene-
" ral of horse, and the Duke of Aveiro, had their
" limbs broken alive. The Duke, for greater igno-
" miny, was brought bareheaded to the place of exe-
" cution. The body and limbs of each of the crimi-
" nals, after they were executed, were thrown upon
" a wheel, and covered with a linen cloth. But when
" Antonio Alvares Ferreira was brought to the stake,
" whose sentence was to be burnt alive, the other
" bodies were exposed to his view; the combustible
" matter, which had been laid under the scaffolding,
" was set on fire, the whole machine, with the bodies,
" were consumed to ashes, and thrown into the sea."

mind on the occasion, were a woman, the old Marchioness de Tavora, and a young man of nineteen years of age, her second son. He had suffered the most cruel tortures without acknowledging his guilt; when his father being brought to tell him that he and the other accomplices had confessed the whole, he replied, " as you gave me life, you may take it from " me." As for the old Marchioness, she escaped the torture on account of her sex; but received her sentence, and saw the preparations for her punishment with an indifference that would have done honour to a better cause. She had been accustomed to breakfast after the English fashion, and after she had heard her sentence read, and been dressed as usual by her women, she demanded her breakfast. Her confessor represented to her that she had something else to do; when she answered, " that " there was a time for every thing." She took her breakfast in perfect tranquillity, and made her women partake of it. When she came to ascend the scaffold, she said to those who offered to assist her, " I will ascend it alone, I have " not suffered the torture like the rest." The Marquis de Tavora, who did not possess an equal strength of mind, reproached her for having brought her family to such a fate; she replied, "support it as I do, and reproach me not." She herself placed the fillet over her eyes, shortened the duties of her confessor, entreated the executioner to dispatch her quickly, and by dropping her handkerchief, gave the signal for the fatal stroke. The young Marchioness de Tavora was confined in a convent, as well as the young Countess of Atouguia, who has been since persecuted by the inquisition as a visionary. The principal part of the nobility were carried away and confined in dungeons, while some escaped; of the latter number were the Almeidas and Sousas. As for the Jesuits, they were expelled from every part of the Portuguese dominions as accomplices in this horrid conspiracy, but without process or proof. There remained of them but twenty-two, decrepit old men, who were shut up in a villa of the Duke d'Aveiro; and eight prisoners, of which the most criminal, viz. Malagrida an Italian, Alexander an Irishman, and Matos, a Portuguese, were executed secretly in prison, after having been denounced as chiefs of the plot.

The Minister has been accused of gratifying, by these executions, his own personal vengeance. But surely this crime merited the severest chastisement; nor could it be considered as bad policy to humble an insolent nobility who insulted the king, and tyrannized over the people.

Since this fatal period, consternation and suspicion have not ceased to afflict the Portuguese: every one sees the sword suspended over his head, and fears the operations of informers and spies. The perpetual seizure of persons, proves that the spirit of persecution has not yet subsided, and the inhabitants have not since this sad catastrophe, enjoyed one tranquil day: the crime is passed, but the punishment continues. The Minister, sure of being detested for his unnecessary cruelty, finds no security, but in keeping alive the general consternation. This cruel necessity has rendered him inattentive to the forms of law, and violent to an extreme in punishment. His power is cemented by the best blood of Portugal, and the title of Count d'Oeyras, which the king has granted him as a recompense for his services, is sealed with the same blood, and purchased by a long series of decapitations.

These two fatal events which followed one upon the other, occupied all the attention of the

Minister, and suspended the operations of every other department of the state, whose strength they had exhausted. War being lighted up throughout all Europe, the Portuguese, who had no interest in it, began to recover themselves and to draw some advantage from the state of peace which they enjoyed. But their neutrality was not equally preserved. They were considered as very much attached to the English; they triumphed on their victories, they received them with joy into their harbours, they profited of their captures, and they were regarded rather as the subjects than the allies of England. This opinion determined the Spanish court to attack Portugal, as the best way of attacking the English, whom they considered as the commercial possessors, at least, of Lisbon and Oporto. It was supposed that this war with Portugal would have a considerable influence on the negotiations for peace; and to accelerate it, Spain resolved to break its neutrality. If Portugal had been subdued, it is certain that such an event would have been the source of great advantage to Spain at the conclusion of a peace; but success alone could justify the conduct which the court of Madrid pursued at this period. That power was particularly interested in preventing the English from aggrandizing their power in America, and crushing the French navy; but this interest did not furnish sufficient motives to quit its neutrality. It might, on all occasions, have favoured the French, have opened their ports to them, and supplied them with money; but they had no just pretence to declare war against England. The piracies of certain privateers, which were disavowed by the court of London, and the strict but lawful examination of Spanish ships which carried ammunition to France, were not sufficient pretexts. All the commercial nations suffered the same inconvenience, without thinking themselves authorized to take up arms to prevent it. Besides these causes of complaint, whether well or ill founded, Spain had nothing to do with Portugal. War was, however, declared in 1762.

The Portuguese, who never thought of a rupture with Spain, were so ill prepared for this unexpected event, that the army was not only in a very bad condition as to discipline, but also as to equipment. The Minister, who was naturally an enemy to military men, because he knew nothing of military affairs; and reckoning upon a long peace, as well as on his own superior politics, he had totally neglected the army, and employed the funds destined for its maintenance, to other objects: he had not even filled up the vacancies in it which had been caused by the late catastrophe.

The state of the Portuguese army appeared on paper to consist of 17,000 men, 2,400 of which were cavalry: but in reality it did not amount to half that number. When the Count de Lippe, a sovereign prince of Germany, who was recommended by the English to command the army of Portugal, wished, on his arrival, to get a body of troops together, in order to have some appearance at least of an army; he could not assemble at his first camp of Villa Viçosa, more than 5000 men; the greater part without uniforms and without arms. Elvas, Almeida, and some other places occupied the rest. There was neither artillery, nor ammunition, nor hospitals, nor magazines, nor engineers, nor officers, nor maps, nor waggons.

Don Martin de Mello had recourse, on the part of the king of Portugal, to the court of London, which ordered 6000 men to embark for Lisbon; 2000 of these were Irish troops, newly raised, consequently as incapable of defending Portugal as the Portuguese themselves, and who arrived when the campaign was half over: Lord Tyrawley, who commanded these succours, was a bad officer, and a very violent man, calculated rather to throw matters into disorder than to restore them. He was the ambassador in Portugal, who made so insolent a use of the favour of King John V. He resumed, on the present occasion, all his haughty, contemptuous airs, and some very warm disputes took place between him and Count d'Oeyras; that Minister, however, contrived to get him recalled. Lord Loudon, who succeeded Tyrawley, Lord Townshend who replaced him, and General Crawford who followed, were equally hated for their pride. They always encamped separately from Count de Lippe, whose orders they refused to receive; in short, they expressed their contempt of the natives so openly, that the Portuguese at length rose up against these cruel and insolent allies, and massacred more than half of them. There was no kind of excess which these undisciplined troops, who were worse than enemies, did not commit. Upwards of 1400 of them perished also in a revolt at Santarem. The Irish, above all, were so disorderly and so wicked, that those who had escaped the vengeance of the Portuguese and returned to England, were broke and punished.

No better service was received from two regiments, called Swiss troops, that the king raised in Portugal; of which one colonel was hung in effigy, while the other died in prison; and the two regiments were afterwards reformed into a single regiment of grenadiers.

The Count de Lippe had also the same difficulties with the Minister, who valued himself much more, and with reason, on his talents for negotiation, than the science of arms, checked all his enterprises, opposed him in every thing, and repulsed the German pride by Portuguese solemnity. The native generals, jealous of the honours which the king shewed to this foreigner, were his greatest enemies.

The Count de Lippe is a prince distinguished by his military talents; and above all by his superior knowledge as an engineer, and officer of artillery. He is haughty, presumptuous, ardent, and leaves much to fortune. He was obliged in Portugal to bend to the various and opposing circumstances that surrounded him, and he there served an apprenticeship to patience. Although he had no opportunity in this campaign to signalize himself, his whole conduct proved him to be an able and experienced soldier.

Such was the interior state of Portugal when the Spaniards penetrated into it. But the Count d'Oeyras not depending upon an armed strength for defence, had recourse to his usual politics. He engaged the Queen to supplicate her mother the Queen Dowager of Spain to dispel the storm which threatened to destroy Portugal. He employed money, he set negotiations on foot, and by these arms, far more powerful than those of the Spanish warriors, caused their enterprizes to miscarry.

Nevertheless the court of Spain ordered 40,000 men to march into Portugal; and from its powers of defence, a ready judgment might be formed of the facility of its conquest. But contrary to all appearance, this army did nothing but what was injurous to Spain itself, by a great and useless consumption of men, of horses, of cattle, of grain, and above all of money. The Marquis de Sarria, colonel of the Spanish guards, old, bigotted, and without talents, was entrusted with the command of this army. But besides the want of vigour and capacity in this superannuated general, the operations of the war were all either checked or impeded by the influence of persons of the highest consideration in Spain. The war Minister was an Irishman,* and all Europe suspected him of partiality for his countrymen. But whatever the cause might be, the preservation of Portugal cost Spain its glory, its treasure, and an army.

The extraordinary ignorance of the Spanish generals, the want of discipline in their troops, the little care that was taken to secure supplies of forage and ammunition, were circumstances very favourable to the safety of Portugal. The enemy entered into the country without having agreed upon a plan of the campaign; and the first encampment was at Zamora, April 21, 1762. They approached the frontier, without being acquainted with the country, without maps, or guides, or spies. A part of the army attacked Miranda, which was blown up by an accident. This conquest determined the Spaniards to enter Portugal on the side of Traz os Montes; and it was then only they discovered that there was a river to pass; but they had neither pontoons or boats, and much time was

* Don Ricardo Wall.

lost in constructing them. May 4, the General being at Alcañisas, said publicly, in speaking of the Portuguese army, " I cannot disco-" ver where these insects are." Bragança, Outeiro, and Chavés, being without a single soldier, surrendered without opposition on the approach of the army.

The General, May 21, sent a detachment against Moncorvo, while O'Reilly, who commanded the light troops, quitted Chavés to get possession of Oporto; which, however, he did not effect: for he was stopped between Villa Real, and Villa Pouça, by 3 or 400 peasants, who drove back his detachment, consisting of 3000 men, as far as Chavés. He owed this defeat to the appearance of fear which he discovered, and which seems to have been common to all the commanding officers detached from the Spanish army.

On the evening of Whitsunday, there was an alarm in the camp; the General ordered all his artillery to be drawn into the rear, that it might not be exposed to the danger of being taken; by which he deprived his army of all the advantage that might be derived from field pieces.

On June 21, an officer, named Alvarez, attacked the village of Freixal, and after having pillaged it, set it on fire. Three hundred peasants, who were shut up in it, and made some resistance, were converted by the gazettes of Madrid into 6000 men. After such a brilliant expedition, the army took the road of Zamora, and it was determined to lay siege to Almeida. On the 4th of August the place was invested; on the 15th the trenches were opened without the least difficulty, as the besieged did not, during the course of the siege, discharge more than four or five cannon. On the 25th the place surrendered, although no breach had been made, nor the first parallel completed. The batteries of the besiegers were at the distance of 1800 feet from the walls, and the siege was attended with the loss only of an ostler, a labourer, and four horses; not one person was wounded during the short time it lasted. There were found in the town ninety-six pieces of cannon of different calibres, all sorts of ammunition and provisions, and 3600 Portuguese, who composed its garrison, all unhurt and in good health. Almeida is a considerable place, and might have stopped the progress of the Spaniards for at least a month; but the governor was fourscore years of age, had been a captain of cavalry in the war of the succession, and was a vain-glorious character. A very able engineer, named Miron, who had thrown himself into the place, was anxious to put it in a state of defence, but the governor having refused to advance the money necessary to carry on the works, a dozen of English and Scotch officers, who were at the head of the regiments in garrison, raised among themselves a very considerable sum for that purpose. But when Miron, on the strength of this subscription, was determined to begin his works, and spoke firmly on the subject, the governor ordered him to be confined in irons, and sent him to be tried at Lisbon. Having, however, deprived himself of his engineer, he retired into his chamber, where he passed all the time of the siege in reciting his rosary. When the English officers ordered the Portuguese garrison to man the outworks, they revolted and refused to obey. Not a single man was seen in the covered way, nor along the curtains during the whole siege, so that no place was ever taken with more ease; and if the Spaniards could have conceived the interior state of the town and garrison, they would not have given themselves the trouble to open the trenches.

After this siege the Spaniards were more embarrassed than before, as to where they were to go, or what they should do. They had calculated that the siege would have occupied the whole campaign, and no further plan had been thought of. Besides, the war was carried on by couriers, and the court regulated all the operations at the distance of an hundred leagues. Old Marquis de Sarria was now removed, and the Count d'Aranda substituted to command the army. This new general made an attack upon Villa Velha, on the banks of the Tagus. Nevertheless, the Portuguese, encouraged by the indecision of the Spaniards, strengthened by the support of the English, and animated by the Count de Lippe, ventured to take the field, and encamped to the number of 12,000 men at Abrantes, and Punhete; while a small camp of Portuguese volunteers, commanded by a brave Scotchman, of the name of Hamilton, and reinforced by two English battalions, and some companies of grenadiers, were posted upon the left bank of the Tagus, opposite Villa Velha, whose castle was garrisoned by three hundred Portuguese. Alvarez had taken this castle without much danger, as it surrendered at the first musket shot. During the march to Villa

Velha, the Count de Lippe had sent Colonel Burgoyne with his English dragoons, and six companies of grenadiers, four of which were Portuguese, to attack Valença d'Alcantara, of which that officer got possession without any resistance, and afterwards pillaged it. Valença is surrounded with walls, and contained a garrison of 1200 militia, under the command of a brigadier general. This affront, however, was soon forgotten by the Spaniards. The capture of Villa Velha had increased the confidence of the detachment of Alvarez, who, despising the enemy, abandoned themselves to a fallacious security. Hamilton perceived their negligence, passed a ford of the river by night with 300 men, half of them English, surprised the camp of Alvarez, consisting of 2000 men, the flower of the Spanish army, spiked their cannon, and repassed the Tagus without loss, leaving behind him no common scene of disorder and confusion.

Such were the transactions of this campaign which finished in the month of September. The Spanish army retired to Alcantara, but at the same time an attack was made upon Campo Mayor, which failed, because the detachment destined to this object arrived with a view to surprise the place at noon-day. The Spanish forces, when they arrived at the frontier, were reduced to 25,000 men, and never did troops experience a more horrible campaign. The sick and the stragglers were almost all of them massacred by the peasants, who were rendered ferocious by the marauding conduct of the Spanish army, and emboldened by the timidity of its generals.

Spain was much more successful in America. Cevallos, the governor of Buenos Ayres, made himself master of the colony of St. Sacrement, and the island of St. Gabriel, which the Portuguese knew not how to defend, and endeavoured in vain to retake; but this advantage did not compensate for the ill-success of the campaign in Portugal; it covered Spain with dishonour, and exhausted her to such a degree as to keep her quiet till the peace.

This war, which might have crushed Portugal, gave it a degree of vigour and elasticity which it did not possess before; and produced a military spirit that still exists, though it received some diminution from the absence of Count de Lippe. The Count d'Oeyras availed himself of these successes, and of the re-establishment of the army, to render himself still more powerful, and to forward his designs.

But the misfortunes of the reign of Joseph I. had not yet ceased. Two years after the war, the customhouse was entirely consumed by fire, with every thing it contained. This was a severe blow on the commerce of the country, many persons were entirely ruined by the event, and many bankruptcies followed. It was said, indeed, that this conflagration was not attended with a general loss, as the most valuable merchandise was in other warehouses, and that the building was purposely set on fire. But be that as it may, commerce must have been severely affected by the accident, and the commercial security of Lisbon considerably diminished.

It has been remarked, that during and since the war, the Portuguese army received very great detriment from the disunion that subsisted, not between the foreign and the native troops, but among the foreigners themselves. The officers were divided into two factions, the English or the Scotch, and the Germans, comprehending also the Swiss and the French. The history of all the trifling disagreements and revolutions which took place in the army of Portugal, would contain a tissue of events disgraceful to the military character; but as the adventure of the unfortunate Graveron, Colonel of the royal foreign regiment, has been mentioned in the different gazettes of Europe, it may satisfy curiosity to give in this place an impartial account of his death.

Graveron, known in France by the name of Peiferrier, was of honourable birth, and first served in the Mousquetaires of France; afterwards a captain of dragoons, he was at length aid de camp of Count d'Herouville, a lieutenant general, who, in 1762, procured him recommendations to Portugal, where the hope of advancing his fortune had led him. The Count de Lippe immediately conceived a regard for this officer, whose social qualities rendered him very agreeable, and made him major of cavalry. The first moments of his advancement were stained by political intrigues, which afterwards gave an appearance of justice to his sad catastrophe.

While Graveron was major of cavalry, there were two regiments in the Portuguese army, which having been raised by two Swiss officers, took the name of their country. The English faction were very violent against the formation of these corps, and their two commanding officers, in consequence of accusations, whether just or unjust I do not pretend to determine, were committed to prison. One of them, named De Saussure, died in confinement, and was afterwards declared innocent; the other, considered as culpable, but a brave soldier, saved himself by flight and was hung in effigy. Graveron, influenced solely by his interest, paid his court to the English, by promoting the disgrace of the Swiss officers; and he received a recompense for his services: the two regiments were formed into one, as I have said already, and given to him. He was very indiscreet in the management of his corps; but he brought on his fate by speaking and writing with too little precaution on the conduct of government. The expences of his regiment was also equal to those of two Portuguese regiments; and that circumstance contributed to his ruin. He was ordered to Lisbon in 1766, where having been arrested with his staff officers, the regiment was disarmed. He was accused of having ill-managed the finances of his corps, of making false returns, and of having changed his name; such were the principal articles of accusation; but they were sufficient, supported as they were by an authority that was irresistible, while his real crimes were his imprudent opinions of the government, and an improper choice of officers in his regiment. As he could not be condemned to suffer death by any military law, the council of war acquitted him. He was, however, farther consigned to the civil judges, who, according to the ancient laws of the kingdom, condemned him to be hanged; which sentence, as a matter of favour, was changed into decapitation. This outrageous and unjust sentence was confirmed by the military judges, who all signed his sentence by order of the king, except Don Bernardo Mello, brother of the ambassador to the court of London, a field marshal, governor of Elvas, and a most upright and humane nobleman. It is very evident, that these proceedings were no more than a pretext to disband the regiment, and the execution of its commander was considered as the most ready way of doing it.

This unfortunate officer was abandoned by the minister of his nation; and the English did not hesitate to speak in the most outrageous terms of that desertion, because they always possess too much consideration for the life of a fellow-citizen, even if he is culpable, to abandon him to the caprice of foreigners.

At length Portugal sustained a shock which made it tremble to its centre. This was the general revolt of Brasil, of which the causes have been deduced in a preceding chapter, under the article Commerce. General Bohm, a creature of the Minister, was sent there with five battalions.

CHAPTER IX.

POLITICAL STATE OF PORTUGAL.

The political state of Portugal may be said to be a state of compulsion; for this nation cannot consult its inclinations, in its enmities or its alliances. The court of Lisbon is attached by necessity, to that of London, is the enemy of Spain, from natural circumstances, and of France, as being the rival of England. The power which possesses the strongest naval force, will necessarily have a predominant influence in the Portuguese government, because the ultra-marine possessions of Portugal, those principal sources of its support, are open to invasion; while neither its navy or its army can administer a sufficient strength to defend them against an enemy who has a superior marine.

It might have been possible at a former period, by engaging Portugal in the family compact, to have rendered a great service to all the southern part of Europe; but the decay of the French navy, and the growing strength of the English, their numerous ships of war, the efficacious succour they have so long afforded to the Portuguese, the ancient and intimate union of the courts of Lisbon and London, the confederation of the courts of Versailles and Madrid against England, have decided the Portuguese to join the party to which their interest directed them, independant of that fear which is the principle of their alliance with the English, of whom they may be rather said to be subjects than the allies. Besides, they have never been suffered to remain neutral; they have been attacked and exasperated; and the disgraceful campaign of 1762, has completed the alienation of their minds from, and added insurmountable obstacles to an alliance with France; of which the unfortunate war in 1757, had already destroyed all possibility. If, however, in a future war the French arms should be more succesful, the Portuguese might be detached from their alliance with England; and being forced, in the first instance, to observe a neutrality, they might be led on to engage in a confederation against that same power which keeps them in *subjection*. It belongs to France to break in pieces the fetters of Portugal, not by negotiations, but by the superiority of its arms.

A good understanding between Portugal, Spain, and France is now become a subject of conjecture: nay, there are those who pretend to foresee an alliance which will destroy the seeds of war. I will suppose such an event, and examine its consequences. The Portuguese would, it is true, always enjoy a partial state of neutrality; but it would be better surely to have them for declared enemies, because a war with them would always prove the means of revenge against England, by causing a considerable diversion of its power; while a simple peace with Portugal would secure the English commerce at Lisbon and Oporto, and deprive Spain of the indemnities which the war might procure it. In short, Portugal must be forced into a complete alliance, or to open war. It must be brought into the situation, to choose decidedly between France and England. Here is the great difficulty. But can it be supposed that the court of Lisbon will abandon the alliance of England, who sustains it, who holds all its factories, is at the head of its companies; on whom it depends to escort the Brasil fleets, or to capture them, to protect their colonies, or to ruin them, to furnish subsistence to Lisbon, or to expose it to famine in blocking up its harbour; who holds the government in its hand from fear, and the nation from interest? What an advantage would Portugal derive from an alliance with France and Spain, who could enable her to repair her losses, and would prevent her ruin.

It is probable, however, that two reasons may influence Count d'Oeyras to direct his negotiations and political sagacity in favour of the enemies of England. 1st. His great age, and his aversion to military men, must naturally produce a wish to terminate in peace his administration and his life, and to amuse the two courts with whom he treats, with the appearance of good-will. 2d. The widowhood of the young emperor which renews the pretensions of Portugal, and the re-union of the two courts which may prove a bar to the views of that of Lisbon, respecting the marriage of the young Infanta. Such are the real motives of the apparent good-will of the Count d'Oeyras, of the good understanding which reigns, and the negotiations which may be proceeding between the three courts.

I do not hesitate to offer my concluding opinion, that force alone can break those treaties which have been cemented by force, and that the enmity or the friendship of Portugal, depends on the success of a future war. Then the Gordian knot must be cut, that cannot be untied.

CHAPTER X.

COUNT D'OEYRAS.

I CANNOT better finish this description of Portugal, than by giving a portrait of this great Minister, who is the creator of it; in whose hands it has recovered its strength, and been restored to that state of good order which it now enjoys. It is an homage which is due to a great man, whom his enemies have blackened, and whom the Spaniards, either from pride or ignorance, do not esteem as he deserves.

Portugal is indebted for its present strength and prosperous condition, to the Count d'Oeyras. He has extricated his country from that state of barbarism, ignorance, and brutality into which it had fallen, and availed himself of the alliance with England, to polish its people, to strengthen its government, and to render the kingdom respectable.

His life is a tissue of extraordinary adventures, which prove the superiority of his genius, and that he was formed to govern.—— Sebastian Joseph Carvalho was born in 1669.

of a noble family of Coimbra. He was educated in the university of that place, where he made great progress in his studies, and distinguished himself by his genius. But being influenced by his passions, and instigated by an irresistible vivacity of temper, he determined upon the profession of arms, and he entered, at a very early age, into a corps of twenty-four archers of the palace guard, in the reign of John V. He there distinguished himself by his talents and courage; but as neither the one or the other would submit to discipline, he committed a variety of follies, and was discharged from that corps. At this period the infant Don Antonio, brother of King John V. a man of a cruel and ferocious character, took great delight in nocturnal combats. The streets of Lisbon were, every night, infested by bands of armed men in search of adventures. The prince, who was the chief cause of all these disorders, frequented the streets at the head of a band of gentlemen, for the pleasure of attacking and insulting the passengers. These armed bands were called Ranchos. A savage emulation possessed all the higher nobility. The Duke de Cadaval, the Marquises of Marialva and Cascaes, the Aveiras and the

Obidos had each their Rancho. The rencounters of these illustrious banditti were every night signalized by wounds and murders, and produced a kind of civil war in the capital, and under the eye of the king. Foreigners formed themselves into leagues offensive and defensive; and under this pretence, sailors came ashore in bodies, attacked the bravos of Lisbon, and robbed them when they were strong enough to effect their purpose.

Carvalho, distinguished for a fine and almost gigantic figure, an uncommon strength, an invincible courage, and handsome countenance, and superior understanding, determined to take the lead of all the bravos of his time. He accordingly associated himself with another young man like himself. They wore white hats and shoes, in order that they might be known in the obscurity of the night, and made a practice of attacking by themselves all these Ranchos, whom they often put to flight, but not without great hazard and frequent wounds. To these efforts of rash precipitate valour, the two champions joined the gallantry of chivalry. Carvalho having captivated the heart of a young lady of the illustrious house of Aveiro, bore her off, and married her in spite of her family; who, considering such an alliance as disgraceful to them, employed all their power to prevent it. Carvalho, for some time resisted all the opposing efforts of that family, escaped from all the ambuscades which they had prepared for him, and braved their poison and their daggers. The Friar Gaspard, who was his relation, alarmed at the fate which threatened him, and foreseeing what he might one day be, sent him to Vienna, as secretary to the embassy. It was in this employment that the talents of Carvalho unfolded themselves. In this interval, he was informed of the death of his wife, who was suspected of having been poisoned by her family. Being thus freed from such a dangerous connection, he had the good fortune to please a lady, who was a relation of the famous Count Daun; but he experienced great difficulty in obtaining her in marriage. The Portuguese ambassador, however, who was the Marquis de Tancos, encouraged his passion, and to remove every obstacle to the attainment of its object, procured the appointment of Carvalho to succeed him in the embassy. In this advancement, the marriage to which he aspired found no further obstruction, and was immediately solemnized. He now began to fulfil the hopes which had been formed of him; his dispatches gained the admiration of the council, who discerned in them that superior political sagacity, that precision and accuracy, which he has since displayed in all the concerns of his administration.

On the death of John V. he was recalled to Portugal, and placed in the council, of which he soon became the oracle and the master. Don Diego de Mendoça his predecessor was banished, and Carvalho possessed himself of the reins of government; nor has there ever been a more stormy or more glorious administration than his. He found himself surrounded by enemies; above all, by the Aveiros, whose destruction he completed about two years since, by imprisoning the last of that family at his return from the vice-royalty of the Indies. All the first rank of nobility, who were full of indignation at seeing the supreme power in the hands of a man only of the second order, formed a league against him. It required all his courage to overcome the dangers that surrounded him, as well from the malignity of his enemies, as from the extraordinary events of his period. But the greater the peril, the more the greatness of his mind discovered itself. In all the storms and tempests which he encountered, he never let go the chain of those designs which he had projected for the good of the state. His universal genius embraced all its departments, attacked every abuse, remedied every evil, tore up every bad root, and planted better. Notwithstanding all the attacks of his enemies, their falsehoods and their calumnies, he must be considered as the restorer of Portugal, which was in extreme danger in 1766, when it was expected he would not survive the illness that afflicted him, but from which he recovered. The king and every good citizen was in a state of real consternation. The most malignant hatred, or a blind prejudice, could alone be insensible to the menaced calamity. To good order, and a plan of government founded in wisdom, anarchy would have succeeded. Portugal, which under his administration had advanced at least half a century, would, on his death, have fallen back to an equal distance. All the various departments of government were now institutions established by him, and would have fallen with him. Unfortunately for Portugal, the Count d'Oeyras is already far advanced in years, and his plans will be ill executed by a successor, even if he should possess the integrity and the understanding to follow them; and it will require at least twenty-five years of the same vigorous efforts, to produce the fruits of his important labours.

This Minister has a passion for writing on abstruse subjects, and borders a little on pedantry. He has personally attacked the Jesuits with his pen, and almost all the various literary works which have appeared within these ten years in Portugal, upon Agriculture, upon the Jesuits, on the College of Nobles, on the Non-infallibility of the Pope, are of his writing. It is impossible but the public business must have suffered, from the time he employed in these trifles, especially at his advanced age.

The Count d'Oeyras is very tall, and possesses a very imposing countenance; he is very witty, and has a storehouse of knowledge. His politeness to foreigners, his amiable demeanour in society, his unalterable resolution, his profound knowledge of politics, his florid eloquence, and his extensive information, may justify the comparing him to Cardinal Richelieu. There is indeed a very striking coincidence in the characters and circumstances of these eminent Ministers. Both of them rose from moderate birth and small fortune to the highest honours. Both of them employed terror as the engine of their government, established the royal authority by cutting off heads, and humbling an insolent nobility. Both of them were ridiculously fond of passing for wits, and men of universal knowledge; both of them were great politicians, imperious masters, irreconcileable enemies, and amiable in society. Both of them attained their splendid elevation by noble means, without paying their court to Fortune, and both acquired immense riches.

The Count d'Oeyras, as well as the Cardinal, is an honour to his nation, as well as the support of it; and from whence he receives the return of hatred and ingratitude; against which he employs, after the example of Richelieu, that resolution and severity which place him above all fear. He found abuse deeply rooted in every department of the state; and he punished without fearing insurrection; he has overthrown the great, and made the brave tremble. He laboured without ceasing, and with an indefatigable zeal, to render his country, by the means of commerce, population, and agriculture, independent of England.

He enjoyed great riches, but they were acquired with honour. His wealth is so immense, that he did not escape the imputation of avarice, from which, perhaps, it is not altogether possible to exculpate him, as his expences were by no means equal to his fortune and his rank. For his personal security, he is always attended by a troop of forty guards, well mounted and armed, which caused an outcry against him, as it appeared extraordinary to see the Minister surrounded by soldiers with their drawn swords, while the King often goes about Lisbon without any guards at all. There are, indeed, no regiments specially appointed to attend his Majesty; but when it is necessary for him to have a military escort, it is formed from the cavalry regiments. This precaution of the Minister, though uncommon, is absolutely necessary in the midst of a nation who are ignorant, superstitious, and mutinous; and whose nobles have always been the principal enemies of the state, are rendered still more dangerous by their cowardly character.

The Minister had by his second wife two sons and two daughters, who resemble him in nothing; and, surprising as it may appear, whose education was entirely neglected. The reputation and splendid character of Count d'Oeyras, will not be establishe till after his death; it will then be complete, and he will be regretted as he ought; because it will be difficult to fill his place with a successor equal to himself. Merit is neither hereditary nor successive, nor is it attached to the office of a minister: on the contrary, its too frequent separation from thence, may be ranked among the calamities of human nature.

THE END.

www.ingramcontent.com/pod-product-compliance
Lightning Source LLC
Chambersburg PA
CBHW032103220426
43664CB00008B/1112